Foundations of Modern Sociology Series

Alex Inkeles, *Editor*

Foundations of Modern Sociology Series

deviance
and control

Albert K. Cohen, *University of Connecticut*

Prentice-Hall, Inc., *Englewood Cliffs, New Jersey*

To NATY, lay sociologist

and connoisseur of deviance.

Prentice-Hall Foundations of Modern Sociology Series

Alex Inkeles, *Editor*

PRENTICE-HALL INTERNATIONAL, INC., *London*
PRENTICE-HALL OF AUSTRALIA, PTY., LTD., *Sydney*
PRENTICE-HALL OF CANADA, LTD., *Toronto*
PRENTICE-HALL OF INDIA PRIVATE LIMITED, *New Delhi*
PRENTICE-HALL OF JAPAN, INC., *Tokyo*

C—20838(p), C—20839(c)

preface

This book looks toward a general theory of deviant behavior—i.e., a system of propositions that are applicable to all the manifold varieties of deviance. Such a theory should account not only for the occurrence of deviance but also for the particular forms that it takes. Whether such a theory is possible or how closely it can be approached only time and hard work can tell. We have many theories about particular kinds of deviance—e.g., crime, juvenile delinquency, alcoholism, prostitution, and so forth, but only a very modest literature that deals systematically with issues that cut across the whole field.

I have made no effort in this book to compile an inventory of the leading theories about this kind of deviance and that. One must, of course, build upon the literature that we have, and much of this book consists of summaries of theories and research about particular kinds of deviance. However, my intention is to offer these as examples of more generalized ways of thinking about deviance, and to emphasize their possible implications for more comprehensive theories of deviance and control.

Again, since we must build upon what we have, this book deals more than I should have wished with those kinds of deviance—crime and delinquency leading the field—that are popularly regarded as serious social problems; these are the kinds that the literature is mainly concerned with. However, it is important that the reader understand (and I have tried to make this clear throughout the text) that deviance, as I use the term, is just as much concerned with the violation of the normative rules or understandings of households, business firms, fraternities, ball teams, committees, and so on, as with "social-problem" deviance, and that all such violations are as much testing grounds for the ideas ventured in this book as are armed robbery and drug addiction.

The reader may be disappointed that I have not dealt at greater length and more systematically with social control, especially with such matters as the rehabilitation of criminals and the treatment of alcoholics. However, I feel that it is difficult to say anything very significant about social control without first saying a good deal about deviance and the more general ways in which control is related to deviance. I have tried to work out the conception of an interaction process within which deviance and control evolve, each responding to the other and helping to shape the other. It is my belief that within such a framework it will be possible to classify and analyze processes of social control in a fruitful way. To have enlarged greatly on such classification and analysis in a book this size would, however, have meant excessive truncation of basic concepts and theories prerequisite to a more sophisticated treatment of either deviance or control.

Albert K. Cohen

contents

deviance,
social organization,
and
social disorganization

one

   The subject of this book is knavery, skulduggery, cheating, unfairness, crime, sneakiness, malingering, cutting corners, immorality, dishonesty, betrayal, graft, corruption, wickedness, and sin—in short, deviance. Deviance, in one shape or another, is everywhere. All societies—the United States of America and the small societies that are your family and mine—have rules, whose violation excites some disapproval, anger, or indignation. And where there are rules, there is deviance. It may be a matter of cheating on one's income tax or cheating on one's wife, of disrespect to the flag or failing to take one's turn in carrying out the trash. Why do so many people insist on behaving in certain ways despite rules to the contrary? Or, to turn the question around: Why, despite the manifest convenience and utility of violating rules, do so many people insist on complying with them so much of the time?

   Our view is that these are two ways of putting the same question, because in order to explain why men behave, we would have to know those circumstances that make the difference between complying with rules and not complying, and in order to explain why men do *not* behave, we would have to know the same. In any case, one way of classifying human actions is in terms of their conformity or nonconformity to rules. There are many other ways of classifying human actions, but insofar as we classify them *this* way and try to develop a theory to explain why actions fall in the one class or the other, we are concerned with a theory of deviant behavior, which is also a theory of conformity.

   To our way of thinking, one way of putting the question is as challenging as the other. However, not everybody sees it that way. Most people, and especially those who think of themselves as tough-minded and realistic, tend to take for granted that it is fairly natural to misbehave and that the real problem is to explain

1

why people conform. Thomas Hobbes, the great English social philosopher, gave the problem one of its classical formulations. Man in a state of nature—that is, in the absence of the bonds of civil society—is governed by reason in the service of his passions. These passions are mainly the desire for gain, safety, and reputation or glory. To these ends men will employ all means, and destroy one another when necessary or expedient. They will relentlessly seek power, and more power to secure that power. They will live, said Hobbes, in a perpetual "war of all against all," and the life of man will be "solitary, poor, nasty, brutish and short."

In the state of nature there are, properly speaking, no right and no wrong, no "conformity" and no "deviance," for there are no laws, no rules, no proper restrictions on man's inborn propensity to take care of his own interests. There is only one solution open to reasonable men, and that is to covenant together and confer on one person or one body of men—*i.e.,* the sovereign—unlimited power to make fitting laws and to compel the subjects to comply with them.

> This is the generation of that great LEVIATHAN, or rather (to speak more reverently) of that *Mortall God,* to which wee owe under the *Immortall God,* our peace and defence. For by this Authoritie, given him by every particular man in the Common-Wealth, he hath the use of so much Power and Strength conferred on him, that by terror thereof, he is inabled to forme the wills of them all, to Peace at home, and mutuall ayd against their enemies abroad.[1]

What keeps men in line is the overwhelming and unlimited power of the sovereign, voluntarily constituted by reasonable men because they well know that this alone will prevent them from tearing one another apart in the pursuit of their several interests.

There are other "tough-minded" theories than Hobbes'. One is to be found in the works of many writers of the psychoanalytical school. According to this view, the "original equipment" of all members of our species includes a bundle of aggressive, destructive energies called the id. The id is not learned; it is just "there." It is impulsive, it presses for satisfaction, it does not stop to think. It is the source of most behavior that we think of as "bad." As we grow up we learn, if we are successfully socialized, to *control* the impulses from the id. These controls are the ego, or the ability to take into account reality, to take pains, to think twice, and the superego or—roughly—the conscience. What we have to explain is *conformity,* and this means to explain the growth and the strength of the ego and superego controls. In the words of Alexander and Staub:

> The criminal carries out in his actions his natural unbridled instinctual drives; he acts as the child would act if it only could. The repressed, and therefore unconscious criminality of the normal man finds a few socially harmless outlets. . . . The only difference between the criminal and the normal individual is that the normal man partially controls his criminal drives and finds outlets for them in socially harmless activities.[2]

What the social contract and the overwhelming power of the sovereign do in Hobbes' theory, the ego and the superego do in the psychoanalytic theory. (We hasten to add that this is *one* psychoanalytic way of looking at the matter. Psychoanalysis is a kingdom of many mansions.)

We will make no effort to multiply instances of this general point of view.

[1] Thomas Hobbes, *Leviathan* (London: Oxford University Press, 1958), p. 132. Italics in original.
[2] Franz Alexander and Hugo Staub, *The Criminal, the Judge and the Public: A Psychological Analysis* (New York: Macmillan, 1931), pp. 34–35.

2

We pause only to point out that both these views are theories of both conformity and deviance, but they are theories in which *deviance is not problematical*, because both theories start from a postulate about human nature according to which the tendency to deviance is given, unless there is impressed upon the organism some counteracting force for conformity.

We will not try to document the contrary view that man is—or at least some men are—naturally good. But we should take note of an observation by the great French sociologist, Emile Durkheim, according to whom morality (doing the right thing) has two characteristics. One is the familiar, even commonplace idea of obligation or duty. But there is more to morality than dreary and reluctant compliance with an onerous sense of duty. The moral is also *good*—that is, *desirable*. We do not just "go along" with morality.

> We find charm in the accomplishment of a moral act prescribed by a rule that has no other justification than that it is a rule. We feel a *sui generis* pleasure in performing our duty simply because it is our duty. . . . No act has ever been performed as a result of duty alone; it has always been necessary for it to appear in some respect as good. Inversely, there is no act that is purely desirable, since all call for some effort.[3]

Durkheim is reminding us that we may get a positive "kick" out of doing good—a lift, an élan, a sense of exaltation from doing the "right" thing. And, as Durkheim suggests, it is not just because the right thing *happens* to be right, and would appeal to us, like a dish of ice cream, whether it were right or wrong. The satisfaction of doing right has something to do with the fact that it *is* right, even if difficult, dangerous, or costly. Sometimes we even seek out, so to speak, moral mountains to scale, and exult in the strenuous climb. Insofar as Durkheim's point is correct, doing right is more than merely succumbing to a superior force, even one that has been "internalized," like a stern conscience. It is attractive in its own right, and it makes as much sense to ask "Why should we do wrong, despite our sense of duty?" as it does to ask "Why should we do right?" The nature of the "charm in the accomplishment of a moral act" is something we shall return to later.

The Functions of Rules

Whatever we may think of Hobbes' argument, he saw one thing clearly: if human beings are to do business with one another, there must be rules, and people must be able to assume that, by and large, these rules will be observed.

Whatever people want—food, clothing, shelter, sex, fame, contract bridge—they must get it by working with and through other people. They must take up positions in organized and complex social enterprises: families, clubs, schools, armies, political associations, ball teams. Each of these may be thought of as a way of fitting together the diverse actions of many people so that the work of the world gets done. But if the actions of many people are to be fitted together, there must be understandings about who is supposed to do what and under which circumstances. Some understandings may be "better" than others in the sense that, if they are followed, they will get the job done better. But the first prerequisite to organized human activity is that there be *some* understandings, however arbitrary they may be. For example, if traffic is to move along the highway, it is less important whether the rule prescribes that people must drive on the right-hand side or

[3] Emile Durkheim, *Sociology and Philosophy* (Glencoe, Ill.: The Free Press, 1963), p. 45.

3

the left-hand side of the road then that there be a rule. The alternative is chaos.

Of course, it does not follow that the rules must provide a blueprint for every human gesture. There is always some room, and often the necessity, for the exercise of discretion or inclination. Every system can tolerate a certain amount of ambiguity, uncertainty, and even confusion, and there are no doubt many rules that regulate conduct with such precision and detail that they thwart rather than facilitate the accomplishment of human purposes. It may be arguable whether any particular rule is necessary or even useful. There must, however, be rules that set *some* limits to discretion and inclination.

However, rules do not automatically translate themselves into action. All rules impose a certain discipline and effort, a subordination of impulse and self-interest to the common understandings. In no human enterprise, whether it be (for example) marriage, business, or politics, can one take for granted that, if he plays by the rules, things will go his way. He may get bored. The costs may prove disproportionate to the rewards. There may be quicker or easier means of getting what he wants out of the game than are permitted by the rules. His participation in one activity may make demands upon his time, his money, or other resources that interfere with his participation in other activities that are more important to him. There are always temptations, therefore, to quit, to give to the activity less of himself than is expected of him, to cut corners, or otherwise to violate the understandings. Every rule, then, creates a potentiality for deviance.

Deviance and Disorganization

Deviance may be destructive of organization in at least three ways. First, it may be analogous to the loss or defect of a critical part in a delicately coordinated mechanism. An organized social activity is such a mechanism, constructed of the coordinated actions of its members. If some of these actions fail to come through at the proper juncture in accordance with expectations, the continued functioning of the larger activity may be impaired or destroyed. So, for example, if the commanding officer of a military unit defects in the middle of a military operation, or if a contractor fails to honor his contract and make delivery of certain essential building materials. However, not all deviance need be destructive of organization; not every defection or broken promise strikes the system at a vital spot. The fact is, almost any system can tolerate a substantial amount of deviance. Vital points—at which deviance deprives the system of one or more essential components—can be determined only by analyzing the organization of the particular activity, and the part played in it by each component.

Then again, deviance may undermine organization by destroying people's willingness to play their parts, to make their contribution to the ongoing activity. It may do this by offending their sense of justice, of the proper ratio between effort and reward. "Idlers," "fakers," "chiselers," "sneaks," "deadbeats," and the like, even if their activities do not directly threaten the interests of the virtuous, offend the virtuous because they share in the rewards, sometimes disproportionately, without undergoing the sacrifices and discipline of the virtuous. It seems unfair. It may provoke bitterness and resentment. And it may undermine one's own determination to play by the rules—or, for that matter, to play the game at all. Just how large a toll in morale, self-discipline, and loyalty to the system is exacted by any given amount of deviance of a particular sort is often impossible even to estimate, no less state with assurance.

But the most destructive impact of deviance on organization is probably through its impact on *trust*, on confidence that others *will*, by and large, play by

4

the rules. After all, each participant to a collective enterprise has committed some resources, foregone some alternatives, made an investment in the future. He has done this on the assumption that, if he plays by the rules, so will others. His effort, whether it be chasing a ball in a baseball game, doing his homework assignment, or showing up on time to an appointment, makes sense only if complemented by appropriate and expected behavior on the part of others. Distrust, even if it is unfounded, weakens organization by undermining motivation; to distrust others is to see one's own effort as pointless, wasted, and foolish, and the future as hazardous and uncertain. One is then inclined to "pull out of the game" if he can, and to invest his resources with those whom he can trust, because deviance, quite apart from its other effects, destroys faith in future performance. Of course, we may be willing to forgive; our sense of injustice may be satisfied by punishing the offender—but deviance may still leave a destructive legacy of distrust.

The critical role that trust plays in all organized social activity is exemplified also in activities that are themselves deviant, such as illegal betting ("bookmaking"). This is an elaborately organized activity, which requires the services of handicappers, who provide predictions of the outcomes of sporting events, on the basis of which odds are determined; of wire services, which instantly relay results to bookmakers all over the country; and of "layoff bettors" or "banking" bookmakers, who take large bets from smaller bookmakers wanting to hedge some of their wagers. If he is to do business at all, the bookmaker must trust these other gentlemen, especially since his claims against them are not enforceable at law. He must also trust that his customers are not themselves involved in an organized kind of activity known as "past-post betting." A past-post betting operation supplies results of horseraces to customers faster than the wire services can supply them to the bookmakers. The customer is then in a position to defraud the bookmaker by placing a bet on a race before the bookmaker knows it is over.[4] Of course, by "trust" we do not necessarily mean faith in the integrity and rectitude of others. Trust may rest on the conviction that others would not dare to violate understandings for very practical reasons, such as retaliation or loss of reputation. Whatever its basis, trust is the indispensable precondition for any viable enterprise, legitimate or illegitimate.

The bookmaker must also trust the honesty of the sporting events on which he is taking bets.

> Goodman A. Sarachan, chairman of the Commission of Investigation of the State of New York, told the subcommittee [of the United States Senate] that a study by his commission of bookmaking betting volume in New York State in 1959 showed the following percentages: horse racing, 42 percent; baseball, 30 percent; basketball, 15 percent; football, 12 percent; boxing, less than 1 percent. "The tiny percentage on boxing is a sorry indication of the low state to which that so-called sport has fallen," he explained. "Even the bookmakers avoid it because of the characters who control it, to whom a fix is normal procedure."[5]

Here we see one "line of business" that has simply not been able to grow (or has perhaps declined from a previously more thriving state) because of pervasive lack of trust.

Again, however, we must qualify ourselves. Although trust is essential to maintain motivation, it does not follow that a social enterprise can tolerate *no*

---

[4] *Gambling and Organized Crime* (Report of the Committee on Government Operations, United States Senate, Permanent Subcommittee on Investigations, 87th Congress, Second Session, Report No. 1310, March 28, 1962), pp. 13–16. (Brackets not in original.)

[5] *Ibid.*, pp. 20–21.

5

distrust. On the contrary, there are few human activities in which we do not take for granted that somebody will try to cut corners or default on his obligations, and we allow for this in our plans. We are almost invariably disappointed by corner-cutters and defaulters, but not always surprised. Department stores and supermarkets take for granted that a certain amount of merchandise will be lost through theft and embezzlement; they allow for this just as they allow for a certain amount of breakage. To a certain extent, they may "insure against" theft by insuring against loss from it—by bonding employees. Many millions of dollars are spent annually for such "fidelity" or "honesty" insurance,[6] one very practical indicator of the essential "normalcy" of distrust. Professors are saddened by cheating and take steps to contain it, but assume as a matter of course that some will succeed at it. Indeed, measures to prevent deviance or to reduce its cost after it has occurred—testimonials to distrust—are integral features of almost all organized social action—government, banking, Little League baseball, *ad infinitum*. Just how far the erosion of trust must proceed before it results in the breakdown of organization cannot be stated in general terms. It depends on the organization, on the position within it of those who are the objects of distrust, on the costliness of the anticipated deviance, on the mechanisms available for restoring trust and providing reassurance (*e.g.*, for "turning the rascals out" and replacing them with persons of undoubted integrity) once trust has been shattered.

Deviance in Support of Organization

It would be a mistake to assume that deviance is necessarily destructive of organization, that it is at best something that the system merely tolerates, or even that it is something that the conforming members of the group want to prevent or eradicate. On the contrary, deviance may, in some circumstances, make positive contributions to the success and vitality of social systems.

Deviance Versus "Red Tape"

By and large, the normative rules that define deviance grow out of the collective wisdom and experience of the group. They provide solutions (although not the only possible solutions) to typical, recurrent problems. For example, the rules of an organization may prescribe procedures for requisitioning supplies: certain multiple forms must be filled out, certain signatures must be obtained, the forms must be submitted through certain channels. These rules usually make sense. They make it possible to keep track of how much of each item is consumed by each branch or department of the organization; to insure that the supplies are being used only for authorized purposes; to budget and plan intelligently for future needs. However, it is in the nature of all rules that they are *categorical*. That is, they anticipate some category of situations, and stipulate the behavior appropriate to that category. However, no two situations which, by the rules, are lumped together in the same category, are identical. However shrewdly the rules have been drawn up, and however well they may be designed for achieving organizational purposes in most of the situations they cover, almost invariably some situations will occur in which conformity to the rules will defeat rather than implement the purposes of the organization. So, for example, a military unit, or the sales office of a manufacturing concern, may encounter some unanticipated situation in which it needs certain supplies immediately and/or in a quantity in excess of its normal quota. If suppliers conform to the rules governing normal quotas and shipping schedules, the materials will arrive too

[6] Norman Jaspan with Hillel Black, *The Thief in the White Collar* (Philadelphia: Lippincott, 1960), pp. 233–234.

6

late and/or in insufficient quantity to do any good, and all parties concerned will be losers. In this case, if the organizational task is to be accomplished, somebody must violate the rules—as in such cases somebody frequently does. It should be noted here that the motivation to deviance in such situations may stem not from a *conflict between* the interests of some individual or sub-unit and the larger organization of which it is a part, but from *identification and concern with* the interests of the larger organization.

A "Safety Valve"

We have observed that every system of social organization imposes a discipline upon its members: it specifies goals they may legitimately pursue and the means they may legitimately employ. However, there are always some persons who, because of their special personal characteristics or their position in the social structure, have wants that the rules do not recognize as legitimate, or are handicapped in their access to the legitimate means of satifying their wants. If the rules are so rigorously enforced that these people are denied all possibility of alternative, albeit illegitimate, avenues to the satisfaction of their wants, and if enough people are so affected, accumulated frustration and discontent may lead to an attack on the rules themselves and on the social institutions which they support. A certain amount of deviance, disparaged but not rigorously repressed, may perform a "safety valve" function by preventing the excessive accumulation of discontent and by taking some of the strain off the legitimate order. For example, it can be argued that prostitution performs such a "safety valve" function with respect to unsatisfied needs, without necessarily threatening the institution of the family. It is not necessary to catalog the economic, reproductive, socialization, and protective functions performed by the family. If the family is to perform these functions, people must be motivated to form families, to adhere to them, and to accept their disciplines. One source of this motivation is a system of normative rules that links the right to regular, dependable, fully respectable satisfaction of sexual needs to the marriage relationship.

Premarital sexual relationships, if they were in no wise condemned or stigmatized, would reduce the attractiveness of the married state and the incentive to marry. Extramarital sexual relationships, if not condemned or stigmatized, would sometimes involve the married party in deep and lasting emotional attachments outside his family. These attachments would compete with his family for his loyalty, affection, and resources, and threaten its stability. However, there is no assurance that sexual interests, and especially the craving for variety, will be satisfied in the marriage relationship. Such assurance is especially lacking in societies wherein marriages are arranged by families. In these circumstances many men, whose freedom of action outside the household is greater than that of women, will seek sexual gratification outside of marriage. There is probably no society in which the family successfully monopolizes the provision of sexual satisfaction.

This extramarital sexual satisfaction, it may be pointed out, need not seriously threaten the family, provided the sexual relationship is defined by both parties and by society generally as strictly a commercial transaction. The relationship is then entirely impersonal—that is, neither party becomes emotionally involved with or attached to the other, and it establishes no basis for any claim of either party on the other beyond "the terms of the contract." Although, more often than not, the man is able to carry on this activity without jeopardizing his social position, the woman who sells her sexual services is stigmatized and degraded. She is not elevated, as a wife would be, to the social status of her sexual partner; neither is she socially acceptable as his consort in public and respectable society. Her pre-

7

dicament demonstrates precisely the characteristic reactions of society attendant upon prostitution. Extramarital sex, confined to this transient, commercial, severely limited, and disvalued kind of relationship, is least likely to reduce the incentive to marry, to threaten the status or security of the wife, or to create bonds of soli-darity that will compete seriously with the obligations of marriage.

Of course the forms of marriage, the structure of family systems, and the varieties of prostitution are exceedingly varied, and this formulation will not apply with the same cogency in all societies. Nor would we argue that prostitution does not have social costs that we have not considered here. However, the argument does suggest that the significance of any form of deviance is not exhausted by an inventory of negative or, as they have been called, "dysfunctional" consequences.[7]

Clarifying the Rules

Normative rules relieve some of the anxiety and uncer-tainty of social interaction by specifying rights and duties, the permissible and the impermissible. To do this job they must be clear to, and understood in the same way by, different participants. However, seldom is the precise meaning of a rule obvious, simply from a verbal statement of it. "Don't take what isn't yours," "Do your own work," "Friends should stand by one another," are very crude indicators of finely shaded understandings. Just what is included within each term of the rule; the exact limits of its applicability; its qualifications and reservations; the intensity of feeling associated with it; whether it is a pious sentiment or an injunction to be taken seriously—all these can seldom be communicated in a few words, or even in a complicated formula. It is a hard fact of life that these things are learned, to a great extent, only by testing the limits (or witnessing what happens when others test the limits) of propriety and *discovering* whether one has overstepped the bounds. Raised eyebrows, chilly looks, social avoidance, amused smiles, nodded approval, may communicate more precisely and forcefully than words the true scope and meaning of a rule. To repeat: whether some disapprove or not, it is only by overstepping the boundaries into the zone of deviance that one really learns what deviance is, and how far and how often he may safely venture into its con-fines.

Pushing the limits and experimenting with deviance does more than play a role in the initial learning of rules; it is also the process through which the group arrives at common understandings. When a rule is newly formulated, it is usually fuzzy around the edges; there is no general agreement on the limits of its applicability. The "trouble case," the event near the borderline, demands of the group that it "make up its mind." Very often, especially when the stakes are high, special institutions are invoked to consider the matter and speak with authority in the name of the group. To reduce the ambiguity of the rules is one of the chief functions of courts of law, especially appellate courts. By providing an occasion for the clarification or reaffirmation of a rule, the deviant may render an important service to the other members of the group: they come to know more clearly than before what they may and may not legitimately do.[8]

Uniting the Group (Against the Deviant)

It has frequently been remarked that nothing unites the members of a group like a common enemy. Competition for wealth, power, status and other values; divergent philosophies; boredom, frustration, and fatigue—all

[7] See Kingsley Davis, "The Sociology of Prostitution," *American Sociological Review* (October 1937), 2:744–755, and "Prostitution," Chapter 6 in Robert K. Merton and Robert Nisbet (eds.), *Contemporary Social Problems* (New York: Harcourt, Brace, 1952), pp. 262–288.
[8] Compare Kai T. Erikson, "Notes on the Sociology of Deviance," *Social Problems* (Spring 1962), 9:307–314.

deviance, social organization, and social disorganization

these drive people apart, undermine morale, and impair the efficiency of the group. An external enemy, who threatens or is believed to threaten what the members of the group cherish in common, arouses the sentiments of the community and revives a waning solidarity. Internal enemies may perform the same function. George Herbert Mead has remarked with reference to the criminal:

> . . . the attitude of hostility toward the lawbreaker has the unique advantage of uniting all members of the community in the emotional solidarity of aggression. While the most admirable of humanitarian efforts are sure to run counter to the individual interests of very many in the community, or fail to touch the interest and imagination of the multitude and to leave the community divided or indifferent, the cry of thief or murderer is attuned to profound complexes, lying below the surface of competing individual effort, and citizens who have separated by divergent interests stand together against the common enemy. . . . The criminal does not seriously endanger the structure of society by his destructive activities, and on the other hand he is responsible for a sense of solidarity, aroused among those whose attention would otherwise be centered upon interests quite divergent from those of each other.[9]

The deviant may, in short, function as a "built-in" out-group, and contribute to the integration of the group in much the same way as do witches, devils, and hostile foreign powers.

Uniting the Group (in Behalf of the Deviant)

The preceding paragraph deals with a special case of a more general phenomenon: the increase in solidarity that results when the members of the group subordinate their divergent interests to pursue some common task. The task does not have to be a hostile response to an enemy; it is necessary only that it be, in the light of the group's values, a task worth doing. It could, for example, be the reclamation of a deviant, or the protection of a deviant from the consequences of his own deviance, or a demonstration of the group's inexhaustible patience and kindness in the face of incessant provocation from a deviant member. The leader of a Quaker work group describes the group's experience with a deviant member:

> X left our group after the first four weeks of the eight-week program. He had never been away from home before although he was about 21 years old. He couldn't seem to adjust to his job at the day camp, and he just couldn't stand doing his share of the housework and cooking. This lack of doing his share was especially hard on us, and we often discussed privately whether it would be good for him to relieve him of any household chores. We decided that wouldn't be right, but we still couldn't get him to work. Funny, but this sort of made housework the center of our group life. We are proud that no one else has shirked his chores: there is no quibbling now. . . . Anyway, X kept being pressured by his mother and brother to come home, but we gave him tremendous support. We talked it all out with him. We let him know we really wanted him to stay. This seemed to unite our group. It was working out the problem of X that seemed to unify our group. It was working out the problem of X that seemed to help us build some group standards. He began to follow some of our standards but he also stayed free to dissent. His mother finally forced him to come home.[10]

[9] George Herbert Mead, "The Psychology of Punitive Justice," in Lewis A. Coser and Bernard Rosenberg (eds.), Sociological Theory: A Book of Readings, 2nd ed. (New York: Macmillan, 1964), p. 596, reprinted from American Journal of Sociology (1918), 23:585–592.

[10] Robert A. Dentler and Kai T. Erikson, "The Functions of Deviance in Groups," Social Problems (Fall 1959), 7:98–107; quotation from p. 103.

This quotation is taken from an article by Dentler and Erikson in which the authors report on a study of the relative effectiveness of ten Quaker work projects in influencing conformity with Quaker norms of tolerance, pacifism, democratic group relations, and related social attitudes. Five of the groups were selected for case study. The two most "successful" groups—those achieving the most change in the desired direction—"had the highest proportions of social isolates, but some of the isolates were low-ranking deviants." [11] The authors conclude that having to do something about the deviants itself contributed to this success. They suggest also that, because deviants perform a variety of functions for the group, the majority will ordinarily strive to keep the deviants within the group rather than to expel them, up to the point where the deviance becomes too dangerous to the group.

The Contrast Effect: Accenting Conformity

The good deed, as Shakespeare noted, shines brightest in a naughty world. Indeed, any valued attribute—moral goodness, strength, wit, beauty—is apparent, draws attention, and is rewarded in proportion as it is set off by the corresponding limitations of others. In a community of saints, goodness is taken for granted; nobody has any special claim to respect, or reason for self-congratulation. Indeed, it may be important to those who behave themselves that there be others who do not. The deviants provide the contrast effect that makes conformity something "special" and a source of gratification. The reader can probably testify from his own experience to the feeling of satisfaction and even exhilaration in talking to some other member of a group about the blemishes and failings of some third party. In censuring another's deviance, we are by implication contrasting him to ourselves and rewarding one another for our superior merit. A certain amount of controlled deviance, then, may provide an anchor or reference point against which conformity can be measured, make conformity meritorious rather than commonplace, enhance the sense of community among the conforming members of the group, and in general contribute to the satisfyingness of life in the group.[12]

A Warning Signal

Deviance may also function as a signal light or warning, inviting attention to defects of organization.[13] Increases in absenteeism from work, truancy from school, AWOL's from the army, runaways and other disturbances in correctional institutions, surly and sullen compliance with orders, and deliberate defects of workmanship, may compel re-examination of existing procedures, reveal unsuspected causes of discontent, and lead to changes that enhance efficiency and morale. The deviant may, by sticking his neck out, thereby render a service to reluctant conformers, who may be subject to the same strains but prefer to suffer them than to violate the rules.

Several years ago the Indiana University faculty had a high rate of violation of campus parking regulations, in part because of the disjunction between the demand for parking spaces and the supply. The virtuous left early for work and hunted wearily for legitimate parking spaces. The contemptuous parked anywhere and sneered at tickets. One response to this situation was to create new parking lots and to expand old ones. Since the new parking spaces were available to all, and not only to the former violators, this provides a clear instance where the

---

[11] *Ibid.*, p. 102.
[12] See Lewis A. Coser, "Some Functions of Deviant Behavior and Normative Flexibility," *American Journal of Sociology* (September 1962), 68:174; Dentler and Erikson, *op. cit.*, p. 101.
[13] Coser, *op. cit.*, p. 174.

10

virtuous—or perhaps the timid—as well as the deviants themselves are the beneficiaries of deviance.[14]

Conclusion

If by "social disorganization" we mean the dissolution of social bonds, the disintegration of social groups, or the disruption of organized social activities, deviance is not to be identified with social disorganization. Deviance, if not contained, is always a threat to organization. In limited quantities and under certain circumstances, however, it may make important contributions to the vitality and efficiency of organized social life, and even the conforming members of the group may neither wish to see deviance extirpated nor the deviant members thrust out. A simple inventory of possible "functions" and "dysfunctions" of deviance such as we have presented here, even if it were complete (which it is not), would be only the beginning of an exploration of the part that deviance plays in the life processes of social systems. Much remains to be done by way of specifying the conditions under which deviance of various sorts has this consequence or that, and at what point the spread of deviance becomes destructive of organization.

[14] Albert K. Cohen, "The Sociology of the Deviant Act: Anomie Theory and Beyond," *American Sociological Review* (February 1965), 30:10. Based on William J. Chambliss, *The Deterrent Influence of Punishment: A Study of the Violation of Parking Regulations*, M.A. thesis (sociology), Indiana University, 1960.

the scope
of the field: I
two

Deviant behavior, we have said, is behavior that violates normative rules. This definition, like most simple definitions, conceals a number of troublesome ambiguities—so troublesome that some sociologists have concluded that it is impossible to reach agreement on a definition and therefore to stake out a field of scientific study called "deviant behavior." But we cannot abandon the field so lightly. The idea of deviant behavior is not an invention of the sociologist; it is a fact of social life: people in society define certain kinds of acts as violations of rules, and certain individuals as rule breakers. Acts and individuals so defined elicit characteristic responses, from gentle ribbing to violent retribution. It is also a fact of social life, and not just a product of sociology's confusion, that there are obscure borderlands between deviance and conformity: people themselves are sometimes unsure of themselves, and sometimes cannot agree on what is deviant. Our effort in this chapter to clarify the meaning of deviance is not, therefore, just an exercise in definition; it is an effort to understand better one of the fundamental ways in which people in society perceive and respond to the world around them.

The Relativity
of Deviance to Roles

The study of deviance cannot be simply the study of drunkenness, narcotic drug use, extramarital sexual relations, prostitution, abortion, and so forth, *as such*, for each of these is, in some society and under some circumstances, socially acceptable. There is no need to discourse at length on the cultural variability in definitions of deviance. Table 1, however, is suggestive of the range of variability with respect to only 19 aspects of sexual behavior. It is based on a study of 110 societies catalogued by Human Relations Area Files, Inc. The types of punishment that were considered evidence of deviation from sexual mores ranged from small fines and parental reproof to torture, enforced suicide, and death. These variations in the seriousness with which the respective forms of deviance are regarded in the various societies are not reflected in the table.

Behavior is deviant, then, only if the actor is subject to the jurisdiction of the rules that the behavior contravenes. This jurisdiction has two distinguishable aspects: collectivity membership, and collectivity roles.

Collectivity Membership

Collectivities are social systems with names and identities to which people are regarded as "belonging." National societies, like the United States or China, are such collectivities. These in turn may contain lesser collectivities like religious bodies, fraternities, factories, families, and gangs. Membership in a collectivity is part of a person's public identity; it tags him as a certain kind of person and regulates people's behavior toward him; in this sense it is a status-position to which is attached a collectivity *role*.[1] Every collectivity has a

[1] On the terms "status-position" and "role," see another volume in this series: Alex Inkeles, *What Is Sociology?* (Englewood Cliffs, New Jersey: Prentice-Hall, 1964), pp. 66–67.

Table 1

Number of Societies Punishing Specific Types of Sexual Behavior

Number of Societies Measured	Percentage Punishing	Type of Behavior and Person Punished
54	100	Incest
82	100	Abduction of married woman
84	99	Rape of married woman
55	95	Rape of unmarried woman
43	95	Sexual relations during post-partum period
15	93	Bestiality by adult
73	92	Sexual relations during menstruation
		Adultery
88	89	(paramour punished)
93	87	(wife punished)
22	86	Sexual relations during lactation period
57	86	Infidelity of fiancee
52	85	Seduction of another man's fiancee
		Illegitimate impregnation
74	85	(woman punished)
62	84	(man punished)
30	77	Seduction of prenubile girl (man punished)
44	68	Male homosexuality
49	67	Sexual relations during pregnancy
16	44	Masturbation
		Premarital relations
97	44	(woman punished)
93	41	(man punished)
12	33	Female homosexuality
67	10	Sexual relations with own betrothed

Source: Julia S. Brown, "A Comparative Study of Deviations from Sexual Mores," *American Sociological Review* (April 1952), 17: 138.

13

set of rules. Part of the meaning of a collectivity role is to be subject to the rules of that collectivity; to claim such a role is to acknowledge that one has become subject to the jurisdiction of the rules of the collectivity. In an interesting way, even individuals who do not themselves belong to the collectivity and who do not approve of its rules take this collectivity membership into account in their judgments of deviance. Thus, for example, non-Catholics may recognize a Catholic as "a good Catholic" or "a poor Catholic" and admire the "good Catholic" for his faithful adherence to patterns of conduct for which they would criticize members of their own religious collectivity. There are also interesting marginal positions—e.g., those of sojourner or guest, whether it be in a household or in a foreign country. Only in a qualified sense are these people "members" of the collectivity that they are visiting; their roles are governed by a special set of understandings which may carry, on the one hand, special obligations, and on the other, special exemptions. They too may be deviant, but only on the terms defined by the rules pertaining to their positions.

Roles Within Collectivities
The members of a collectivity are in turn differentiated according to their positions within the collectivity, such as "foreman," "teacher," "parent." With respect to such positions we may always ask: What are the expectations or rules that go with the position? Who has a valid claim to the position? Let us illustrate by reference to categories of persons that we do not ordinarily think of in terms of "positions" and "roles." One example is the "sick" person.[2] The criteria of the position—what it takes to be "sick"—vary somewhat from culture to culture. For example, a wide range of conditions that are called "mental illness" in our culture are not recognized as illness in others. To claim the sick role successfully—or to have it thrust upon one—others must be persuaded that one's condition meets the current criteria of the corresponding position. However, there is hardly anything that is more difficult to communicate to others than the precise quality and intensity of one's aches, pains, weakness, and lethargy; it is quite possible to be sick without any visible symptoms or special discomfort; and the boundaries between sickness and well-being, according to the current criteria, may be uncertain. It is understandable that people are often reluctant to take one's word for it that one is sick, and thereby to incur the special obligations that one has toward a sick person. Indeed, the individual himself is often unsure whether he is unwell enough to be sick and may strive, despite his pain or weakness, to play the role of a well person. One of the important functions of the medical profession is to certify, when title to the role is uncertain, to sickness, as an I.D. card certifies to age. They settle the question, in an impersonal and efficient way, of whether one is sick and whether one is a minor, respectively, and thereby the question of what rules he is subject to. In this way they help to avert what could otherwise be awkward social situations.

As a *bona fide* sick person, one is entitled to exemptions from the rules that would ordinarily apply to him; he is also subject to expectations that ordinarily would not apply. He is entitled to a certain sympathy, support, and consideration from others. At the same time, he must "follow doctor's orders," "try to get well," be a "good patient," and not exploit his illness by making "unreasonable" demands on others. He is not deviant by virtue of being sick; however, he is now capable

[2] Talcott Parsons, *The Social System* (Glencoe, Ill.: The Free Press, 1951), pp. 433–447; Robert N. Wilson, "Patient-Practitioner Relationships," in Howard E. Freeman, Sol Levine, and Leo G. Reeder (eds.), *Handbook of Medical Sociology* (Englewood Cliffs, N.J.: Prentice-Hall, 1963), Chap. 11; Samuel W. Bloom, *The Doctor and His Patient* (New York: Russell Sage Foundation, 1963), Chap. 4.

14

of being deviant in ways that only a sick person can be deviant. Furthermore, the sick role engenders rights and duties not only for the sick person but for all the members of his "role set"—doctor, family, friends, fellow workers—and new ways in which they too can be deviant. But it must again be emphasized that these are condoned only if he is socially defined as sick. As Bloom observes:

> If Mr. Jones, a bookkeeper, appears late one morning, and he is flushed and leaves his desk frequently, he may, without any penalties, go home early if he convinces his employers that he is "sick." If, on the other hand, Mr. Jones has a hangover from too much drinking the night before, he may feel sick, but it is not likely that he will be granted the privileges of the sick role.[3]

Much the same can be said of the role of the "bereaved" person. When somebody dies, people take it for granted that certain of his kith and kin will grieve. The signs that constitute sufficient evidence of grief to justify the claim to the bereaved role are culturally variable. In some cultures one must cry inconsolably. In others it is sufficient, or better, to go around with a somber expression and a "stiff upper lip." In any case, if the outward expression is accepted as evidence of the necessary inner emotional state, the normative rules relative to the bereaved role are activated. Like the rules governing the sick role, they provide opportunities for deviance to both the bereaved person and to the members of his role set. Finally, if the bereaved person is discovered "having fun" or enjoying himself in ways that are considered incompatible with his claims to bereavement, he may forfeit the role of the bereaved person altogether, and all the exemptions that pertain to it. Indeed, he is now guilty of a type of deviance that is everywhere regarded with a special odium. He has claimed an identity that he does not really have, like impersonating a doctor, a married person, or a sick person. To make such a false claim is to force other people to take up and play the correlative roles, to subject themselves to a certain discipline, to go through elaborate and sometimes stressful motions that turn out to be meaningless and "don't count." It is a flagrant violation of trust.

Role Conflict

Each position that a person occupies brings him under the jurisdiction of a particular set of rules or "role-expectations." If these rules make contradictory demands on him, it may be impossible, or possible only at great cost, to conform to them all. Conformity relative to one rule may necessitate deviance relative to another. Such contradictory demands arising out of one's role-expectations are called "role conflict." [4]

Melvin Seeman has described a number of such conflicts in the roles of the school superintendent. Superintendents are expected to work for higher salaries for their teachers. They are also expected to interact informally and democratically with their teachers. Seeman obtained from school teachers in 26 communities "separatism scores" which were essentially measures of the extent of informal interaction between teachers and their superintendents. He also obtained data on financial trends in the same schools and communities.

> . . . one of the most striking results was the positive correlation . . . between the superintendents' "separatism" (as described by the teachers) and the amount

[3] Bloom, op. cit., p. 113.
[4] See Harry M. Johnson, Sociology: A Systematic Introduction (New York: Harcourt, Brace, 1960), pp. 22–39.

of salary increase obtained for the teaching staff over a three year period. In short, where salaries went up there was high leader separatism.

If we assume, as our superintendent evaluation suggests, that the prevailing teacher code condemns superintendent separatism, and, of course, approves salary increases, we find apparently that the superintendent is placed in the unenviable position of being asked to engage in two behaviors which do not "go together." In order to achieve salary increases, he presumably must spend his time not with subordinates, but with those superiors and community influentials who wield power. As one superintendent succinctly put it: "You don't visit your classrooms regularly because you're writing publicity for the next levy that you can't have fail. It must pass. Therefore, you don't know what is going on in the classrooms too well."

Yet the normative code, it seems, asks him to do both, and though the trend is against it, some superintendents do succeed in achieving both salary increases and low separatism. It is interesting to speculate on the toll which success exacts in mental health or in long run administrative efficiency. That there are such tolls is not a matter of pure speculation, for the sense of tremendous pressure as a result of joint school and community demands runs through many of the interviews with these same superintendents.[5]

Role conflict may arise out of contradictory demands within the same role relationship as in the instance just described, among different relationships within the same role set, among different roles that the same person plays in the same social system, or among the roles that he plays in different systems. Whether two rules are in conflict depends not on the rules alone but also on other properties of the system. For example, two roles may make incompatible demands, but the system may be so organized that no individual is likely to play simultaneously that particular pair of roles. The role of "examination proctor" and "friend" may make quite different demands, but they come into conflict only if the same person finds himself in both positions at once.[6] Role conflict is therefore a source of deviance that is inherent in the structure and rules of the system itself—in other words, a structural source of deviance. (We considered another, but closely related, structural source of deviance in the last chapter when we discussed how the rules themselves might block the attainment of organizational objectives, and thereby build up pressure to circumvent or violate the rules.)

Validity and Propriety

We must, in speaking of deviance, specify the system of reference and the roles to which the rules apply. The real difficulties arise when we ask: Who is to say what the rules are? Even within the same system, men do not agree on what is knavery, skulduggery, cheating, stealing, etc. Are some men's opinions worth more than others? Shall we settle the question by counting noses? What, in short, are "the rules of the system"?

First, however, we should not lose sight of the fact that the area of agreement may be broader than we sometimes think. After all, disagreements are the things that people are noisiest about. We should not allow this noise to drown out the broad areas of agreement—sometimes so taken for granted that we are not even conscious of them. Nor does the fact that the rules are often honored as much in the breach as in the observance alter the fact: we all do things we concede are "wrong."

[5] Melvin Seeman, "Role Conflict and Ambivalence in Leadership," *American Sociological Review* (August 1953), 18:373–380. Quotation from p. 376.
[6] See Samuel A. Stouffer's classical study, "An Analysis of Conflicting Social Norms," *American Sociological Review* (December 1949), 18:707–717.

Much of the disputation about rules is over the question of what the rules *ought to be* rather than over what they *are*. We may disagree on the *propriety* of a rule—that is, on whether it is a good, fair, reasonable rule—but agree on its *validity*. This is not a trifling distinction. To concede the validity of a rule is to concede that people have a right—even an obligation—to use it as a standard of judgment and to apply sanctions to those who violate it. I may think that the speed laws in my city, or the rules about smoking in classrooms on my campus, are silly, but I recognize that they are valid rules; this recognition implies at least that the "proper authorities" have the right to enforce them if I violate them. This is a distinction of great practical consequence for social systems, for there is a lot of room for disagreement about the propriety of rules without upsetting the smooth workings of a social system. There is little room, however, for disagreement about what the rules *are* if people are to live and work together. This is why one of the most important features of a social system is the understandings people have about how rules acquire the stamp of validity—that is, about how, notwithstanding different notions about what the rules ought to be, some rules come to be recognized as *the* rules in force, the "rules we go by," the rules entitled to the backing of constituted authority.

This distinction is applicable to social systems of every scale, from legislative bodies to engaged couples. Men who disagree vigorously on what the laws ought to be, at least agree on those procedures by which *proposed* laws become *the* laws. A couple who disagree on the wisdom or necessity of some understanding—*e.g.,* whether a certain piece of information should be kept a secret between the two of them—may nonetheless agree that that *is* the understanding because on such-and-such an occasion they "promised" to treat it as a secret. It is when the criteria of validity themselves break down that the basis of organized social action disintegrates.

This does not mean that differences with respect to the propriety of rules are inconsequential. Much has been written about the ineffectiveness of rules of law that run athwart of the community's sense of fitness and propriety, or—to put it in other words—that are out of joint with those less precise and uncodified rules that we call the folkways and the mores, and that provide a framework for evaluating the propriety of the legal rules. The argument has sometimes been overworked; "respect for law" confers upon legal rules a powerful authority, even over those who believe them to be unjust. But certainly rules lose much of their ability to command compliance if they are resented as unjust, and the sense of propriety becomes an important factor in accounting for deviance. The significance of validity and propriety are well illustrated by Harry V. Ball in his study of rent-control violations.[7]

In 1952, landlords in Honolulu were legally bound not to charge more rent than the maximum established by one of three legal procedures, the procedure depending upon the time of construction of the housing unit and the time that it first came under rent control. These procedures were intended to be fair to both landlords and tenants. However, as it turned out, these procedures did not to the same degree take account of the general postwar inflation. Harry V. Ball analyzed the responses of the landlords of 1,068 rental units to a questionnaire asking each landlord to state precisely what rent he believed would provide him a fair return. This was compared with the legal maximum rent as indicated for his unit in the Rent Control Commission's files. As expected, the proportions evaluating their ceiling rents as unfair varied with the procedures used in fixing the rent. From the procedure which made the least allowance for postwar inflation

[7] Harry V. Ball, "Social Structure and Rent-Control Violations," *American Journal of Sociology* (1960), 65:598–604.

to that which made the most, the percentages were 70.4, 53.6, and 40.3. At the same time, at least one adult tenant of each rental unit was interviewed to determine the rent actually paid and the services actually offered. From this it was possible to determine for each of 1,050 units whether it was a violation or nonviolation of the rent-control regulations. The percentage of violations for the three categories in the same order were 29.2, 14.9, and 7.3. The percentages of violations according to the landlord's evaluation of the ceiling are given in Table 2.

Table 2

Percentage Distributions of Ceiling Violations and Nonviolations by Landlord Evaluations

Evaluation of Ceiling	Violations	Nonviolations	Total
Fair	——	34.0	26.4
Don't know	——	4.2	3.3
Unfair	92.5	54.6	63.0
No response	7.5	7.2	7.3
Totals (%)	100.0	100.0	100.0
Totals (N's)	232	818	1,050

Source: Harry V. Ball, "Social Structure and Rent-Control Violations," *American Journal of Sociology* (1960), 65: 603.

The most striking observation is that not one "fair" response is located in the violation category. There can be no doubt that the sense of unfairness is an important determinant of violation. On the other hand, 54.6 per cent of the nonviolations also involved an evaluation of the ceilings as unfair, so this of itself was apparently not enough to induce a violation. It should be noted that the study distinguishes carefully between general attitudes toward rent control and attitudes toward the specific ceilings that are established. In the questionnaire each landlord was asked, "Do you believe rent control in Honolulu is necessary at the present time?" There was no relationship between violations and the responses to this question. The mere fact then, that one disagrees with the necessity of a law does not mean that he feels free to violate it. The study as a whole serves to remind us that the sheer fact that a rule has been established according to certain recognized procedures confers upon it a certain validity and moral authority quite distinct from that conferred upon it by our recognition of its necessity; that if the rule is felt to be unjust or unfair in its specific applications, the barriers to violation are greatly reduced; and that, finally, even then violation is by no means assured.

Aberrant and Nonconforming Behavior

The distinction between validity and propriety reminds us of a related distinction, made by Robert K. Merton, between two classes of deviant behavior, "aberrant behavior" and "nonconformity." The aberrant violates the rules but neither disputes their validity nor tries to change them; he is more interested in getting away with his violation than with doing anything about the rule iself. Most of those whom we ordinarily think of as "criminals" would fall in this category. The nonconformer, on the other hand, "aims to change the norms he is denying in practice. He wants to replace what he believes to be morally suspect norms with ones having a sound moral basis." Therefore, whereas the aberrant hides his deviance, the nonconformer seeks to draw attention to what he believes to be imperfect norms by openly flouting them. In short, the aberrant is commonly assumed to be acting out of self-interest; the non-conformer out of disinterested reforming zeal.[8] The different aims give rise to different styles of deviance. Of course, even the nonconformer may recognize the validity of the rule whose propriety he denies and which he is trying to replace. Should he, however, deny the criteria of validity themselves, he is withdrawing from the rules the last shred of legitimacy. The *rebel* is neither aberrant nor nonconformer; he does not merely quarrel with the wisdom of this or that rule, but denies the very authority on which the claim to validity of a whole set of rules rests. Luther was an abominable heretic in the eyes of the Catholic Church, not so much because he wanted to change some of the rules, but because he denied that promulgation by the Pope conferred upon them any special validity:

> Therefore [he wrote] it is a wickedly devised fable—and they [the Romanists] cannot quote a single letter to confirm it—that it is for the Pope alone to interpret the Scriptures or to confirm the interpretation of them. They have assumed the authority of their own selves. . . . Only consider the matter. They must needs acknowledge that there are pious Christians among us that have the true faith, spirit, understanding word, and mind of Christ; why then should we reject their word and understanding, and follow a pope who has neither understanding nor spirit? Surely this were to deny our whole faith and the Christian Church. . . . We should gain courage and freedom and should not let the spirit of liberty (as St. Paul has it) be frightened away by the inventions of the popes; we should boldly judge what they do and what they leave undone by our own believing understanding of the Scriptures, and force them to follow the better understanding, and not their own.[9]

When differences reach this point, the last bit of common ground has indeed been washed away.

Institutionalization

There remain those situations in which there is no clear-cut answer to the question, "What are the rules of the system?"—because there is, as a matter of social fact, no consensus on what the rules are. And because there is no consensus, some people, stigmatized by others as deviant, refuse to accept this definition of themselves. Those rules whose authority and validity are unquestioned, we speak of as "institutionalized." [10]

Perfect institutionalization is the exception. In a heterogeneous, rapidly changing society, there are few rules whose validity somebody does not deny and whose application is not regarded as an illegitimate attempt on the part of some to enforce their predilections on others. We must emphasize again that we are not

---

[8] Robert K. Merton and Robert A. Nisbet (eds.), *Contemporary Social Problems* (New York: Harcourt, Brace, 1961), pp. 725–728. Quotation from p. 726.

[9] Martin Luther, "Address to the Nobility," tr. by C. A. Buchheim, in *The Harvard Classics* (New York: P. F. Collier and Sons, 1910), Vol. 36, pp. 284–285. (Brackets added.)

[10] Our use of this term is closest to that of Talcott Parsons in his *The Social System* (Glencoe, Ill.: The Free Press, 1961), p. 39. For Parsons it signifies the degree to which normative expectations are *shared* and to which people feel *committed* to their fulfillment. The term also connotes the degree to which rules are formally spelled out and backed by sanctions. See Harry M. Johnson, *Sociology: A Systematic Introduction* (New York: Harcourt, Brace, 1960), p. 20; and Inkeles, *op. cit.*, pp. 67–68. Since these various characteristics do not always vary together and in the same direction, we find it necessary to make it explicit that we are using it primarily in the sense of "sharedness."

speaking of Merton's "aberrant," who does not dispute the validity of the rule he violates. We are speaking of those who refuse to accept the critical judgment of others because they deny the rule on which the judgment is based. If the rule has become codified into law, they either deny the right of the law to extend its rule over this behavior, or insist that there is some "higher law" that takes precedence. Thus some homosexuals, some people who have recourse to illegal abortion, some adherents of extreme and proscribed political groupings, and some marihuana users refuse, whatever the law or "public opinion" may have to say about them, to accept the definition of their behavior as violations of valid rules, and the definition of themselves as deviant.

Even where institutionalization is imperfect, however, one rule or set of rules is usually dominant. By this we do not mean that more people believe in it, although usually they do. We mean rather that some rules enjoy a certain respectability that their rivals do not: they may be freely and publicly assented to; they represent the folk wisdom of the society and require no defense; they are the rules that are publicly recognized, if not always observed, by respected public figures; they are the common sense of the solid citizen. Those who dispute these rules are seen as *and tend to see themselves as* "outsiders." They may be powerfully convinced of the rightness of their views, but they are on the defensive. Openly to espouse their beliefs is unsafe; it invites trouble. The insiders need not be circumspect; they know that all sensible people agree with them. The outsiders can speak freely only in "off-beat" groups of the same persuasion. If they can speak out publicly at all, it is uneasily and defensively. They may know they are right, but they also know that it is *their* beliefs that are "strange." [11]

Thus, in the American system, not only the homosexual, but he who would defend homosexuality as "all right," is an outsider; the conscientious and convinced atheist, and especially the outspoken atheist, is an outsider; the regular marihuana user who is an insider of the "cool" world still sees himself as an outsider relative to the world of "squares," [12] and it is clearly the squares who represent the "main stream" of American society.

As we move still farther from the pole of perfect institutionalization, we arrive at the point where no rule is clearly dominant. At this point two groups— each confident that it is in the main stream, neither feeling that it is an outsider— confront one another; or there may be no clear alignment of groups, but just a general uncertainty about what precisely the rules are and how far the limits of the permissible extend. Thus, at one time those who defended boy-girl dating with a certain amount of kissing and fondling were clearly the outsiders; today they are the insiders, and the former insiders are "old-fashioned" and "prudes." (At some point, of course, the rising curve of the one camp and the declining curve of the other crossed, and it would have been impossible then to say whose represented the dominant, "insider," position.) The increasingly common pattern of boys and girls embracing and nuzzling one another in the corridors of academic halls is, at this moment, of uncertain status. It is still on the defensive and therefore not yet dominant, although it appears to be indicative of the wave of the future.

This discussion does not imply that, as we move away from perfect institutionalization, the concept "deviance" becomes less meaningful and less useful. We still have people defining others as deviant; important consequences still flow from such definitions; and we still have to explain the *occurrence* of behavior, notwith-

---

[11] Howard S. Becker uses the term "outsider" synonymously, it seems, with "rule-breaker." See his *Outsiders: Studies in the Sociology of Deviance* (New York: The Free Press of Glencoe, 1963), Chap. 1. We are pointing out that even those who deny the validity of the rules, even though they do not violate them, may be defined as "outsiders."

[12] *Ibid.*, Chaps. 3 and 4.

standing that it is so *defined*. What this discussion does imply is that, as consensus on the rules declines, we must become increasingly careful to specify *whose* conception of the rules we are, at the moment, working with. It also implies that, since deviance depends as much on the existence of a rule as on the occurrence of an act, deviance may be created or expunged by changes in rules. Therefore, the explanation of deviance must be as much concerned with origins and changes in rules as with the behavior that the rules forbid.

Deviant Individuals and Deviant Collectivities
                 In the literature of deviant behavior it is usually taken for granted that deviant acts are always the acts of individuals. This probably reflects an underlying assumption that super-individual entities or "collectivities" are fictions or illusions; as such, they cannot "do" things, and only individuals can really commit acts. From the point of view of everyday life, however, it is equally taken for granted that collectivities—corporations, countries, universities, fraternities, armies, lodges, ball teams, trade unions—*are* real and that they *do* do things, many of them deviant: they break contracts, they commit atrocities, they cheat, they violate laws, they do mean, sneaky, and treacherous things. The "man in the street" also fears, hates, loves, admires, attacks, and defends them, in much the same way that he does individuals. This "man in the street" includes philosophers and sociologists, when they are not engaged in writing books or lecturing on the nature of reality. They do not doubt that "the gas company" overcharged them or that "the university" is not paying them what they are worth. (Whether collectivities are real is an interesting and important metaphysical question; as sociologists, however, we do not have to—and won't—become involved in metaphysical arguments.)

If we apply the label "actor" to any object that is socially defined as an agent—as something to which people attribute attitudes, decisions, actions—then collectivities are actors. Of course, to "see" a collectivity and to see it "doing" things is not just a matter for the eyes in one's head. A collectivity as a thing in its own right comes into existence when people organize themselves in accordance with a particular scheme or pattern of relationships. To "see" the collectivity one must be able to see the correspondence of an actual set of relationships to such a pattern. And to do this, one must have the pattern as part of his mental equipment. The culture of each society equips its members with many such patterns; each pattern defines a different type of collectivity. Corporations cannot misbehave in Australian aboriginal society, nor clans in ours, because the patterns that define these kinds of collectivities are absent in the respective cultures.

But the culture does more than lay down through these patterns, the conditions that a structure of social relationships must meet in order to constitute a collectivity of a certain kind. It also includes the criteria on the basis of which people attribute acts to collectivities, as distinguished from the several and distinct individuals who are its members. These criteria may be implicit and intuitive, as when the man in the street says of some country that "it" has wantonly attacked some other country, that a mail order house has misrepresented a product in its catalog, or that a political organization has engaged in subversive actions. In other cases the criteria are more formal and explicit. For instance, a very precise set of rules stipulates when a legislature has passed a law or a fraternity has admitted a member.

Of course every collectivity act is the outcome of an interaction process among a plurality of individuals, although one single individual might make the crucial decision or physically perform the deed. The question, however, is: When is an individual seen as doing something in his own right and when is he seen

21

as speaking or acting "in behalf of" or "in the name of" the collectivity? The criteria of which we are speaking are the rules we implicitly or explicitly follow when we make such distinctions, and these rules are culturally variable. An interaction process may also culminate in an attribution of acts to both a collectivity and to certain members of the collectivity. For example, following a drowning during a fraternity hazing, culpable acts may be attributed to the fraternity and also to certain of its members; or, a corporation may be found guilty of violation of the antitrust act, and certain of its officers pay for their special contributions to this collectivity offense.

Although these questions about the attribution of actions to collectivities may seem somewhat recondite and abstract, they are in fact equally applicable to the attribution of action to individuals. This is also dependent on cultural criteria and is similarly culturally variable. Mr. Jones drops a banana peel on a sidewalk and Mr. Brown slips on it and breaks a collarbone. Did Mr. Jones do anything to Mr. Brown or was it an "act of God"? A woman pays some thugs for doing away with her daughter-in-law. Did the woman kill her daughter-in-law? A man succumbs to the deliberately provocative enticements of a fifteen-year-old girl and has sexual intercourse with her. Has he raped her? These are the kinds of questions that arise in the criminal courts.[13] The answers depend on the criteria for attributing agency in the particular legal system.

Such questions arise, however, not only in courts of law but in the courts of public opinion, and there, too, the answers vary from society to society and from time to time. *In general*, social events are the outcomes of interaction processes, to which different people contribute in various ways. Whether the event is defined as an act at all, whether it is attributed to an individual or a collectivity, and what sort of an act it is, are culturally patterned ways of interpreting experience.

Collectivity deviance, then, has the same claims to consideration as does individual deviance. One can study the causes of collectivity deviance, its rates, and its distributions. The explanations will require analysis of the interaction processes that culminate in events socially defined as deviant acts of collectivities. These explanations will be related (though in complex ways that are not well understood because they have been so little studied) to explanations of individual deviance. The work of Edwin H. Sutherland on "white collar crime"[14]—chiefly the violation of federal statutes by business firms—is one of the few systematic studies of the crime rates of collectivities, and even it does not clearly distinguish collectivity deviance from individual deviance.

If deviant acts are attributed to collectivities, the consequences are different than if they are attributed to individuals. One cannot, of course, horsewhip a corporation, or put a university in jail. But both may suffer penalties, ranging from public disgrace to forced dissolution—a kind of corporate "execution." Or they may suffer deprivations—e.g., fines—that are absorbed by the total membership. The American Association of University Professors investigates charges against colleges and universities; if it finds them "guilty" of—for example—violations of rules of academic freedom and of tenure, it "censures" them. Such a censure imposes very real disabilities, including loss of prestige, and reluctance of teachers to accept positions in the censured institutions.[15]

Finally, the individuals who are members of these collectivities have stakes in the "good name" of the collectivity. Since their membership in the collectivity

---

13 See Richard C. Donnelly, Joseph Goldstein, and Richard D. Schwarz, *Criminal Law* (New York: The Free Press of Glencoe, 1962), pp. 523–660.

14 Edwin H. Sutherland, *White Collar Crime* (New York: Dryden, 1949).

15 Detailed and documented accounts of proceedings against colleges and universities may be found in any issue of the *AAUP Bulletin*.

the scope of the field: I

is an important part of their public identity—both the meritorious achievements and the disgrace of the collectivity attach, in some measure, to them—they have an interest in restraining one another from behavior that might result in the attribution of deviance to the collectivity. In this way, the processes of social control *within* the collectivity are intimately related to the attribution of deviance *to* the collectivity.

In this chapter we have gone part way in staking out the field of deviant behavior. In order to clarify the meaning of "deviant behavior," we have discussed its dependence upon collectivity membership and positions within collectivities; we have addressed the difficult question of "What are the rules of the system?"; we have introduced the concept of institutionalization and the distinction between validity and propriety; and we have defined deviant behavior to include both aberrance and nonconformity, and the deviant actions of both individuals and collectivities. In the next chapter we shall continue to spell out the kinds of inquiry with which the sociology of deviant behavior is concerned.

the scope
of the field: II
three

It is one thing to commit a deviant act—*e.g.*, acts of lying, stealing, homosexual intercourse, narcotics use, drinking to excess, unfair competition. It is quite another thing to be charged and invested with a deviant character—*i.e.*, to be socially defined as a liar, a thief, a homosexual, a dope fiend, a drunk, a chiseler, a sinner, a criminal, a libertine, a rate-buster, a brown-noser, a hoodlum, a sneak, a scab, and so on. It is to be assigned to a role, to a special type or category of persons. The label—the name of the role—does more than signify one who has committed such-and-such a deviant act. Each label evokes a characteristic imagery. It suggests someone who is *normally* or *habitually* given to certain kinds of deviance; who may be *expected* to behave in this way; who is literally a bundle of odious or sinister qualities. It activates sentiments and calls out responses in others: rejection, contempt, suspicion, withdrawal, fear, hatred. To commit the deviant act is not necessarily to acquire the deviant character. Say for instance that a child lies or steals or destroys property. If his deviant behavior is made known, he may be socially defined as "basically a good kid," as acting "out of character," as "a wild kid," as "mixed up," as "a juvenile delinquent," as "a young criminal," and so on, or as some combination of these. But if his deviance does not come to light, the situation may provide no occasion for the assignment of a social character, deviant or otherwise. Of course, it is also possible to acquire a deviant character on the basis of false or erroneous accusation.[1]

[1] Howard S. Becker, *Outsiders: Studies in the Sociology of Deviance* (New York: The Free Press of Glencoe, 1963), pp. 19–22.

From Deviant Actions
to Deviant Characters

All things considered, it is clear that deviant actions and deviant characters are "horses of different colors"—closely related but quite distinct from one another. This distinction and others to be discussed below—e.g., differences in visibility and in official status—must be taken into account in collecting and interpreting data about deviance.

The Prevalence of Deviance

People who commit deviant acts—let us call them *offenders*, to distinguish them from deviant characters—are not a sinister minority of underworld inhabitants. Even if we limit the term to people who, at one time or another, violate the criminal law, most of us are offenders. One of the first studies to dramatize the prevalence of deviance was that of Wallerstein and Wyle.[2] They distributed questionnaires listing 49 offenses under the penal law of the state of New York. All these offenses were sufficiently serious to draw a maximum sentence of not less than one year. (Although the sampling was not rigorously scientific and the results are not to be taken as accurate indicators of the prevalence of criminality in the larger population, these questionnaires give convincing evidence that the law violator is Everyman. Subjects were requested to check each offense they had committed, and indicate whether they had committed it before the age of 16, the upper limit for juvenile court jurisdiction in the state of New York. Questionnaires were returned by 1,698 individuals— 1,020 men and 678 women, mostly from the New York City metropolitan area. Ninety-nine per cent admitted committing one or more offenses. The percentage of individuals admitting to specific offenses, excluding those committed as juvenile delinquencies, is shown in the following partial list. The table must be interpreted judiciously. Some of the acts reported might be technically criminal, but would not ordinarily lead to criminal prosecution—for example, some fist fights that would appear here under "assault."

The mean number of different offenses committed in adult life by men ranged from a low of 8.2 per person for ministers to a high of 20.2 for laborers, with a mean of 18 for all men. For the women they ranged from a low of 9.8 for laborers to a high of 14.4 of those in military and government work, with a mean of 11 for all women. The men reported a mean of 3.2, the women 1.6 of juvenile offenses. Although data are not presented on this matter, it is to be presumed that very few of these offenses ever came to police or judicial notice.

Similar conclusions may be drawn from numerous other studies on "hidden offenses."[3] It does not follow that there are no differences between "hidden" and "official" offenders. On the contrary, those who find their way into court are, *on the average*, likely to have committed more different offenses, to have committed

---

[2] James S. Wallerstein and Clement J. Wyle, "Our Law-abiding Law-breakers," *Probation* (March-April 1947), 25:107–112, 118.

[3] James F. Short., Jr., "The Study of Juvenile Delinquency by Reported Behavior: An Experiment in Method and Preliminary Findings," paper read at annual meetings of the American Sociological Society, 1955 (mimeographed); Austin L. Porterfield, *Youth in Trouble* (Fort Worth: Leo Potishman Foundation, 1946); Edward E. Schwarz, "A Community Experiment in Measurement of Delinquency," *National Probation and Parole Association Yearbook* (1945), pp. 157–181; Fred J. Murphy, Mary M. Shirley, and Helen L. Witmer, "The Incidence of Hidden Delinquency," *American Journal of Orthopsychiatry* (1946), 16:686–696; Maynard L. Erickson and LaMar T. Empey, "Court Records, Undetected Delinquency, and Decision Making," *Journal of Criminal Law, Criminology, and Police Science* (1963), 54:456–469.

Table 3

Percentage of Men and Women
Admitting Various Criminal Offenses

Offense	Men	Women
Malicious mischief	84	81
Disorderly conduct	85	76
Assault	49	5
Auto misdemeanors	61	39
Indecency	77	74
Gambling	74	54
Larceny	89	83
Grand larceny (except auto)	13	11
Auto theft	26	8
Burglary	17	4
Robbery	11	1
Concealed weapons	35	3
Perjury	23	17
Falsification and fraud	46	34
Election frauds	7	4
Tax evasion	57	40
Coercion	16	6
Conspiracy	23	7
Criminal libel	36	29

Source: Wallerstein and Wyle, op. cit., p. 110.

more serious offenses, and to have committed the same offenses more frequently.[4] But the overlap between the two populations is substantial and impressive. In brief, we are all offenders, but we differ in the patterns into which our offenses fall. These patterns differ according to the number of different offenses committed, their frequencies, and the specific combinations in which they appear. Some offenses no doubt have an affinity for one another. They tend to come in bundles, or some lead to others in a characteristic progression. A number of studies have found scales, clusterings, or patterns of deviant actions, and have attempted to devise theories to account for them.[5]

Visibility and Identification

From the commission of a deviant act to the acquisition of a deviant character may be either a long road or a short one. First of all, the act must become socially visible to somebody other than the perpetrator. The range of visibility may be limited to the party or parties to the act; it may include narrow circles of intimates, confidants, family, or bystanders; it may extend through circles of ever widening radius to virtually the whole society. Of course, the fact

[4] Short, op. cit.

[5] F. Ivan Nye and James F. Short, Jr., "Scaling Delinquent Behavior," American Sociological Review (1957), 22:326–331; Lester F. Hewitt and Richard L. Jenkins, Fundamental Patterns of Maladjustment (Springfield, Ill.: Thomas, 1947); Albert J. Reiss, Jr., "Delinquency as a Failure of Personal and Social Controls," American Sociological Review (1951), 16:196–207; John F. Scott, "Two Dimensions of Delinquent Behavior," American Sociological Review (1959), 24:240–243; James F. Short, Jr., and Fred L. Strodtbeck, Group Process and Gang Delinquency (Chicago: University of Chicago Press, 1959).

the scope of the field: II

that an act does not come to the attention of "constituted authorities"—e.g., acts of cheating to the attention of professors and deans, or theft to the attention of the police—does not mean that they are not visible to somebody, and that that visibility does not have serious social consequences. An act of infidelity known only to the husband, the "other woman," and the wife might wreck a marriage. However, as the studies we have cited suggest, the range of visibility in most cases is small, and adverse consequences to the offender either absent or trivial. The staff of the Institute for Sex Research at Indiana University analyzed interview data from a sample of 5,293 white, nonprison women. Of these, 51 reported a total of 68 *legal* abortions, but 531 reported a total of 1,044 *illegal* abortions. In only a little more than 3 per cent of the cases of illegal abortions were unfavorable social consequences reported, and none of these represented trouble with the law.[6] It is to be presumed that the social visibility of these illegal abortions is negligible.

Table 4

Percentage of Offenses Cleared by Arrest, and Disposition of Persons Arrested, 1963

Offense	Offenses known, cleared by arrest [a]	Persons arrested, charged by Police [a]	Persons charged, found guilty of same or lesser offense [b]	Persons charged, referred to juvenile court [b]
Murder and non-negligent manslaughter	91.5	77.2	66.7	6.5
Forcible rape	72.2	79.2	49.3	19.2
Robbery	41.0	79.7	51.8	30.6
Aggravated assault	74.4	85.9	49.2	13.6
Burglary–breaking or entering	26.6	84.0	40.7	49.9
Larceny-theft	18.8	82.5	46.1	41.8
Auto theft	26.8	87.0	30.6	57.8

Source: Adapted from *Uniform Crime Reports—1963* (Washington, D.C.: Federal Bureau of Investigation, 1964), Tables 10 and 11, p. 97.
[a] 1,679 cities: 1963 estimated population 52,329,000.
[b] 1,787 cities: 1963 estimated population 51,695,000.

We must also distinguish between the social visibility of offenses and of-fenders. Even of offenses known, only a certain fraction are linked to offenders, and the knowledge of offenders may range from the slightest suspicion to abso-lute certainty—which still does not preclude error. In other words, visibility is not a matter of range only, but also of clarity and certainty. In official criminal statistics the distinction between offense and offender is reflected in the distinc-tion between "crimes known to the police," on the one hand, and "persons ar-rested" or "crimes cleared by arrest," on the other. The latter expression refers to offenses for which somebody has been arrested who is considered by the police as a good enough suspect to warrant "clearing the books" of the case. Table 4, based on data gathered by the Federal Bureau of Investigation from cooperating police departments, shows, for seven major crimes, the percentages of crimes known that were subsequently cleared by arrest. It also tells us how many arrests were followed by formal charges, how many of those charged were found guilty in the criminal courts, and how many were referred to the juvenile court. (The outcomes

[6] Paul H. Gebhard, Wardell B. Pomeroy, Clyde E. Martin, Cornelia V. Christenson, *Pregnancy, Birth and Abortion* (New York: Harper, 1958), pp. 194, 196, 208.

27

of cases referred to the juvenile courts are not known because of the confidential nature of juvenile-court proceedings—a special device to restrict visibility of offenders to parties directly involved, and the personnel of the court). We may think of the successive stages of the legal process as representing, on the whole, increases in clarity and certainty of offender-identification. However, as clarity and certainty increase, the percentage of "survivors" from the total population of offenders decreases.

We must further note the great variability in the ways in which different offenses and offenders are affected by the screening process. As we have seen, the fraction of illegal abortions that become "crimes known to the police" is minute. Murders, on the other hand, have a high probability of becoming known to the police. Moving on to clearances, if we summarize all seven offenses listed in Table 4, offenses cleared are 24.1 per cent of offenses known. The percentages for individual offenses, however, vary from 91.5 per cent for murder and non-negligent manslaughter to 18.8 per cent for larceny-theft. Furthermore, the high percentage for the former category is based on the small figure of 2,340 cases known to the police; the small percentage of the latter figure is based on the large figure of 836,629. Similar variability may be observed in the subsequent stages as well.

The factors accounting for this variability are numerous. We will mention only a few.

(1) Some offenses have, in the ordinary sense of the word, no victims to lodge a complaint or raise a hue and cry. Such are most of the so-called "vices"— e.g., illicit sexual relations between willing partners, or the use of forbidden drugs.

(2) Where there is a victim, and the offender is known to him, he may come to a private settlement with the offender, rather than press the case. For example, a large but unknown percentage of cases of theft, and other property offenses, are settled by compensation to the victim and do not go beyond the stage of arrest, if they reach that stage at all.

(3) The victim may refrain from publicizing or pressing the case because he cannot do so without bringing shame or embarrassment to himself—e.g., blackmail and rape.

(4) Some offenses (e.g., armed robbery and sexual assaults on children) arouse the moral indignation of the community more than others (e.g., illegal gambling and fraudulent advertising), resulting in differential pressures on enforcement agencies to discover and punish offenders.

(5) Offenders may be organized to buy off or otherwise neutralize detection and enforcement agencies—e.g., large-scale syndicated crime.

Within each class of offenses and of those who commit them, different individuals and groups have different probabilities of becoming visible and publicly identified. Almost every text and monograph on crime and delinquency discusses the way in which such variables as age, sex, race, economic status, and "connections" might affect the likelihood of a person's becoming a police or court statistic.[7] There is also an increasing literature on the way in which the interaction between offenders and enforcement agents affects the decision of the latter to push a case to the next stage.[8]

The Uses of Official Statistics

These considerations affecting prevalence, visibility, and identification have two quite distinct kinds of implications.

[7] See, for example, Marvin E. Wolfgang, *Crime and Rare: Conceptions and Misconceptions* (New York: Institute of Human Relations Press, The American Jewish Committee, 1964).
[8] See Irving Piliavin and Scott Briar, "Police Encounters with Juveniles," *American Journal of Sociology* (September 1964), 70:206–214.

First, insofar as we are interested in the occurrence and distribution of deviant acts and offenders, they raise methodological problems. What are the rates of different sorts of deviance? What are the patterns into which they fall? How are particular kinds and patterns of deviance distributed within the population? What are the characteristics of offenders? Our principal sources of data are the records maintained by agencies charged with enforcement; they are the bookkeeping records of "business transacted" by police, courts, correctional institutions, regulatory commissions, and the like. But we have seen that these records are not complete registries of offenses and offenders. They describe—incompletely and not without error at that—only those that have become visible in various degrees to legal agencies. Each provides us with a *sample* of a population we are interested in, but we do not know what fraction the sample is of the respective population. Furthermore, each sample is *selective* and *biased* in different ways, so that it is difficult to make confident inferences. We can correct for bias to some extent if we take pains to become knowledgeable about the ways in which these records are compiled, but we are always left with considerable uncertainty. We can also try to devise new ways of obtaining data, such as the sampling and interviewing techniques of Kinsey and his associates, or the administration of anonymous questionnaires to selected samples or sub-populations. But there are no easy solutions. We must do the best we can, and then be guarded in the inferences we draw.

But we may be interested in the records and doings of official agencies for other reasons than their utility as clues and indexes to the total population of offenses and offenders. We are also interested in the social processing of deviance; in the ways in which, out of the total population of deviant acts and actors, some become visible, identified, and selected for specific kinds of handling. To be caught cheating on an examination; to be recorded on a police blotter; to be convicted of a crime—and the further consequences of such exposure—are events significant in themselves. Therefore official statistics, the records of "business transacted" by official agencies, may be used as bases of inference about the largely invisible total populations of offenses and offenders, or as data for the study of the later processing of these populations by agents of social control.

The Transformation from Offender
to Deviant Character

Even to be identified as an offender, whether it be in the world of the courts or in the extra-judicial world of everyday life, is not necessarily to acquire a deviant character. In 1949 Edwin H. Sutherland published his famous study of white-collar crime. This was an analysis of the crimes committed by 70 of the largest manufacturing, mining, and mercantile corporations and their subsidiaries, over the period of their "life careers." (The average "life career" was 45 years.) The offenses studied included misrepresentation in advertising; infringements of patents, trademarks, and copyrights; rebates; financial fraud and violation of trust; and other offenses committed by businessmen in the course of their occupations. Most of the offenses were not decisions of criminal courts but were findings of independent commissions, such as the Interstate Commerce Commission, the Federal Trade Commission, and the Federal Food and Drug Administration. However, these commissions are public bodies charged with the administration of laws; their procedures are quasi-judicial in nature; their findings are published together with the evidence and testimony, and the decisions recorded by Sutherland related only to acts that were defined as criminal in the statutes. The total number of decisions against these corporations was 980 and the average per

29

corporation was fourteen. Sixteen per cent of the decisions were made by criminal courts, and the seventy corporations had an average of four convictions each.[9]

These offenses are matters of public record, although, as with other types of offenses, they are but a small fraction of the obscurely visible or totally invisible offenses. Although their monetary cost to their victims cannot be estimated, the cost of a handful of cases of financial fraud and misleading advertising can run to many millions of dollars. Generally, however, in cases of white-collar crime, neither the corporations as entities nor their responsible officers are invested with deviant characters—though in some sensational cases they do acquire unsavory reputations and the roles of villains. As a rule, the public images of the corporations are not significantly damaged, and their officers continue to be substantial and respected citizens of their communities.

Schwarz and Skolnick [10] questioned 58 physicians who had been parties to medical malpractice suits. Regardless of the outcome—whether they had won, lost, or settled out of court—their practices were unaffected. Apparently the public character of a physician is not easily tainted. By contrast, however, the same investigators presented each of 100 employers with information about a person seeking unskilled, handyman-type work. Although the employers believed he was a *bona fide* applicant, he was in fact fictitious. One out of 25 employers who were informed that the candidate had been tried and convicted for assault indicated a willingness to consider hiring him. But even those employers who were presented with a letter from a judge certifying a finding of not guilty and reaffirming the legal presumption of innocence were measurably affected by the fact that the candidate had been accused and tried. In sum, the reputations of the physicians appear to have remained undisturbed; the handymen have become, at least, "suspicious characters." Furthermore, the study makes clear that one can become enough of a "suspicious character" to seriously jeopardize his job opportunities even if he has committed no offense at all.

Occasionally it is urged that the proper concern of the sociology of deviance is limited to the processes whereby offenders become identified, and individuals acquire deviant characters. The argument for this position is that deviance enters meaningfully into people's lives, and becomes something to which people can respond, only when it is socially imputed to particular individuals; in particular, it has no consequences for the later career of the offender if he is not visible to others as an offender. Deviant acts need not, however, be linked to particlar offenders to have significant consequences. Successful and undiscovered deviance may lead to further experimentation with it. Deviance may create emotional problems for the offender even if it is unknown to others. On a broader (societal) scale, a vast apparatus of social control and enormous expenditures of energy are directed to the prevention and discovery of deviance that never becomes visible or never becomes linked to particular offenders. One need only think of the social machinery for controlling cheating in examinations and for preventing young people from engaging in forbidden sexual activities. All this police-type activity is not a reaction solely to the tiny fraction of identified offenders; it is a reaction to the widespread and well-founded belief in the prevalence of hidden deviance and unidentified offenders—most of which, despite all this prodigious activity, remains hidden and unidentified. It is important to appreciate the distinction between deviant actions, deviance of various degrees of visibility, and deviant characters, and that the explanation of one is not necessarily the explanation of the others.

[9] Edwin H. Sutherland, *White Collar Crime* (New York: Dryden, 1949), Chaps. 2 and 3.
[10] Richard D. Schwarz and Jerome H. Skolnick, "Two Studies of Legal Stigma," in Howard S. Becker (ed.), *The Other Side* (London: The Free Press of Glencoe, 1964), pp. 103–117.

The Sociology
of Normative Rules

In our discussion of institutionalization we remarked that since it depends as much on the existence of a rule as on the occurrence of an act, deviance may be created or expunged by changes in rules. The study of the making and unmaking of rules is, therefore, an intrinsic part of the study of deviance. Such a study might focus on the content of a particular body or system of rules— e.g., the criminal law, the law of courts martial, the rules and regulations of bureau-cratic organizations, the "professional ethics" of an occupational group, or the normative understandings, usually more implicit than explicit, of small social systems like families or children's gangs. It might, on the other hand, focus on a particular category of behavior—e.g., homosexuality or "combinations and con-spiracies in restraint of trade"—and the different ways in which it is treated in different systems of rules. The sociology of normative rules is concerned with both those rules which define deviant acts or offenses, and those which define deviant roles or characters. Finally, it distinguishes between two aspects of the "meaning" of a rule, which are necessary to distinguish because they may, to some degree, vary independently of one another. These are the *criteria* of the class of actions or actors defined by the rule as deviant—that is to say, the characteristics that determine membership in the class; and the *pragmatic meaning*—that is, the feelings and actions that the labels denoting these classes call out in people.

Some Illustrations
of Normative Variation

Some of these distinctions are illustrated by the ways in which the deviant behavior of young people has been treated .in English and American law. As far as the world of the courts is concerned, the "delinquent child" was invented in 1899, when the first juvenile court was established in Cook County, Illinois. To "qualify" as a delinquent child, one must meet the criteria laid down in these statutes, including those of age and sex, and of course that of implication in the commission of certain kinds of offenses. The young people al-leged to be delinquent are not subjected to the criminal courts, with their public proceedings and punitive philosophies; it is thought more proper that they be handled by a separate set of courts as "wards" of the state, and by special pro-cedures. The juvenile courts are charged with acting *in loco parentis*—in the place of the parent—and with making such dispositions as, in the judgment of the court, serve best the interests of the child as well as of the community. The child may be "found to be a delinquent child," but he is not "convicted of a crime" and he is not to be incarcerated with "criminals."

During most of the history of the English and American legal systems, how-ever, the distinction between "crime" and "delinquency" did not exist. Young people who were believed to have committed acts forbidden by the law were either held to be too immature to be responsible for their acts, in which case they could not be judged by any court; or they were indicted for their crimes and tried in the criminal courts just like adults, and if found guilty were subject to the same punish-ments. *There were young criminals, but there were no delinquent children.* The two categories are distinguished today not because young people are different from older people, but because we have come to feel that this difference *makes a differ-ence*, one large enough to warrant different treatment. When, from some large class of behavior or persons, we split off a segment that is now felt to be different and to call for different treatment, we are likely to create a new terminology signify-

31

ing two kinds of "things" where before there was one. Thus a new category of deviance is born, with its own criteria or boundaries, and its own pragmatic meaning.

However, the term "delinquent," like the term "criminal," is not just a legal designation. It also has meaning in that unwritten system of rules that we may call "the social code of everyday life." Not only the criteria but also the pragmatic meanings may differ importantly in these two systems of rules. To be delinquent at law may mean that one must report to a probation officer and observe the conditions of probation; to have the extra-legal role may mean that one is denied admission to certain social circles and regarded with distaste by "nice" people. Which set of consequences hurts more is an open question.

We have touched only lightly and by way of illustration on a few aspects of a complex subject. We have not mentioned the distinctively sociological problem: to account for the changes, inside and outside the law, of the normative rules affecting the conduct of young people. What changes in the structure of society, in cultural conceptions of human nature, in the status of young people, and in the relationships between the generations, have produced the changes in the normative rules? One can speculate. For example, F. Musgrove has shown how, over the past hundred years or so, young people have become progressively separated from responsible and productive roles in the economic system, increasingly segregated from the serious concerns of the adult world, and increasingly dependent upon adults.[11] Does the emergence of the juvenile court, with its attendant conception of the diminished responsibility of young people, and the increased responsibility of adults toward the young reflect in the field of the law this more general and pervasive transformation in the relationships between "adults" and "children"? We do not know because, although there is a large literature on the *history* of the legal status of young people, the distinctively *sociological* question has seldom been put, much less seriously pursued.

By contrast to "juvenile delinquent" and "delinquent child," there are other deviant roles that once were important but have ceased to operate as socially recognized categories. Such for example is "heretic," one who deliberately upholds a doctrine at variance with that of his church. Our world is full of people who fit this criterion, but rarely do we *label* them heretics, or *see* heretics when we look at them, or *feel* toward them the special abhorrence supposedly reserved for heretics. As a part of our mental equipment the category "heretic" is almost, although not altogether, extinct. It is still occasionally revived and put to work in the Roman Catholic Church, but even here the pragmatic meaning is very different from what it once was.

Variation among subgroups of the same society with respect to the criteria of a deviant role may be illustrated by reference to the concept "homosexual." The question here is not the pragmatic meaning of the term, but the question, "Who is a homosexual?" Albert Reiss,[12] on the basis of extensive interview data, points out that to engage in sex relations with a person of the same sex may or may not make him a homosexual in American society. It is not uncommon among lower-class, street-corner boys to engage in *fellatio* (mouth-genital sexual relations) with adult males in exchange for monetary payment. In everyday argot, to engage in *fellatio* makes one a "queer" of a particularly obnoxious kind. However, in this lower-class world, if a boy does it only casually and sporadically; if it is incidental to his primary involvement in, and attachment to, the street-corner group; if he does not take the "passive" or "feminine" role in the act of *fellatio*; and if his

[11] F. Musgrove, *Youth and the Social Order* (London: Routledge and Kegan Paul, 1964).
[12] Albert J. Reiss, Jr., "The Social Integration of Peers and Queers," *Social Problems* (1962), 9:102–120. Reprinted in Becker (ed.), *op. cit.*, pp. 181–210.

the scope of the field: II

fellows are persuaded that he does not do it because he derives satisfaction from it but only to obtain some ready cash; he is not marked out as a special sort of person, "different" from other members of his group. He is not stigmatized; he does not acquire a deviant character. *He is neither a queer nor a homosexual.* From the point of view of respectable middle-class folks, however, it is another story altogether. Reiss' research represents a close look, as it were, at a small patch of an enormous territory, the field of intra-societal variations in the normative regulation of sexual behavior. Like most of the work that has been done in this field, however, it is concerned with the discovery and documentation of this variation and of its consequences, rather than the explanation of the normative variation itself.

The Sociology of the Criminal Law

Attempts to account for variation in normative rules have dealt mostly with provisions of the criminal law. We will present two contrasting examples of approaches to the sociology of the criminal law.

(1) P. A. Sorokin [13] sees a society's legal system as one of many cultural sectors, along with its philosophy, art, literature, religion, and so forth. The particular items that go to make up each of these sectors, and the several sectors themselves, are not a random collection but are "logico-meaningfully integrated." By this Sorokin means that at the core of each culture there is a set of "fundamental premises" which constitute that culture's assumptions about the nature of reality, man, the good, and the source of truth. All compartments of a culture embody these assumptions: they are logical implications from the same premises or expressions of the same meanings. On the basis of their fundamental premises, cultures tend to fall into three main types—ideational, idealistic, and sensate. Very briefly and much too simply: the ideational is otherworldly, deeply religious, and contemptuous of the flesh, and exalts faith above reason or the testimony of the senses. The sensate is very much this-worldly; it exalts empirical science and places high value on the satisfaction of man's appetites and material interests. The idealistic represents a balance between the two. According to Sorokin, Western society is presently in a rather "overripe" sensate period. As the premises themselves change, all compartments, including the criminal law, change accordingly—not piecemeal or randomly. The coordination or integration is not perfect, first because each compartment has a certain "margin of autonomy," so that some achieve a certain stage or move out of it before others do; and second because there are other, albeit secondary, factors that do not operate equally on all compartments. However, in the main, the criminal law of a society will express the same underlying values and beliefs that other compartments of the culture do.

Sorokin's test of his theory is but one part of a much larger work and is parallel to independent tests of the same general ideas applied to each of the several sectors of culture. He distinguished 104 main types of actions which have been considered criminal at one time or another during the history of Western legal systems. For each of five countries (France, Germany, Austria, Italy, and Russia) he determined which of these were present in the earliest code available (usually dating from the early Middle Ages), and examined each subsequent main code, noting offenses that have been dropped and added. (In addition, he analyzed changes in the range of behavior brought under the definition of each crime; variations in the intensity of punishment; and other data with which we shall not be concerned here.) The presumption is that the premises of the culture

[13] See Pitirim A. Sorokin, *Social and Cultural Dynamics* (New York: American Book, 1937), Volume II, Chapter 15, "Fluctuation of Ethicojuridical Mentality in Criminal Law." This chapter is written in collaboration with N. S. Timasheff, and can be properly understood only against the background of the general theory developed in Volume I.

33

mentality will largely dictate what sorts of things will be considered offensive enough to be made criminal. Sorokin concludes, indeed, that his data demonstrate precisely this, and thus support what is not only a theory of the criminal law but a general theory of culture. Thus the medieval codes, expressive of an ideational or idealistic culture mentality, dealt severely with sensual self-indulgence and offenses against religion, whereas as we moved into the more modern and sensate era, the law tended to protect people in the enjoyment of sensual and creature comforts, and to deal lightly with offenses against religion.

If the reader should turn to the detailed exposition in Sorokin's text, he may find himself questioning some of that author's characterizations of culture as a whole, and of specific cultural products in terms of his main types. There are extremely difficult methodological problems in achieving objectivity and consensus on the description of the "spirit" of a "culture mentality" and on the "logico-meaningful" harmony or disharmony of two cultural elements. However, Sorokin's study remains unique and challenging in its scope, its historical sweep, and its attempt to unify a multitude of findings in a grand, theoretical synthesis.

(2) Howard Becker [14] uses the Marihuana Tax of 1937—which we shall get to shortly—to illustrate a process which he suggests is applicable to rules in general.

It may be obvious, but it deserves restatement, that laws do not just come into existence when they are "needed" or "wanted." First of all, according to Becker, somebody must have a strong enough *interest* in the enactment of the law to take the initiative and press for its passage. Such persons, he suggests, can be called "moral entrepreneurs." They make it their business to sew another patch onto the moral fabric of society.

One kind of work that has to be done is to persuade others that the law serves some recognized value of the society. Values are highly generalized statements about what is good or desirable, but their specific implications for conduct in specific situations do not necessarily follow obviously. Somebody must derive these implications, or find some values from which these implications may be derived, and then defend their derivations against alternative derivations. The work also includes *publicity*—the arousal of a large enough segment of important and influential opinion to a sense of the urgency of the proposed legislation. It further includes the *neutralization* of the objections of others whose interests will be adversely affected by the proposed law (if indeed they are sufficiently motivated and sufficiently organized to create an effective opposition).

Becker illustrates this process by citing the passage of the Marihuana Tax Act of 1937—ostensibly a revenue measure but so drawn that except in very special circumstances the sale, purchase, or possession of the drug is a serious crime. The passage of this act is of special interest for two reasons. (1) Although marihuana produces a kind of intoxication, it is not a drug of addiction—*i.e.*, it does not produce a physiological dependence; it does not produce any serious organic impairment or deterioration; and there is no good evidence that it contributes significantly to the commission of crimes. In all these respects it is incomparably less damaging than the use of alcohol. Although there were *state* laws against marihuana prior to 1937, marihuana use was generally not regarded as a serious social problem and the laws were laxly enforced.[15] In short, we are not dealing here with the spontaneous recognition, on the part of Congress, of a self-evident evil. To create the necessary feeling of urgency and alarm, sustained and large-scale moral entrepreneurship was necessary. (2) Most of this entrepreneurship came from a single

[14] Becker, *Outsiders: Studies in the Sociology of Deviance*, Chap. 7.
[15] See Alfred R. Lindesmith, *The Addict and the Law* (Bloomington: Indiana University Press, 1965), Chap. 8.

the scope of the field: II

agency, the Federal Bureau of Narcotics, a division of the United States Treasury Department.

Becker does not speculate at length on why the Narcotics Bureau developed such a strong interest in the passage of this legislation. We may assume that its officials were genuinely convinced that they were waging war against a fearsome and destructive enemy, but this does not tell us why they felt that way. The answer to this important question can probably come only out of a close study of the history of the Bureau. It is probable that it is linked to the fact that the Bureau had long been charged with the enforcement of the Harrison Act, directed at the traffic in opiate drugs, which *are* drugs of addiction, and that it had acquired considerable prestige as the nation's bulwark against the evils of "dope." Any enlargement of its operations and consequent further enhancement of its reputation required the identification of new public enemies. Marihuana lent itself readily to this role, first because it could be represented as a "dangerous drug," and second because the organization and skills the Narcotics Bureau had already built up in dealing with opiate drugs could be readily turned against marihuana. Any organization—a government bureau, an industrial firm, a university—seeking new worlds to conquer or new ways to be of service, tries to capitalize on the equipment and expertise that it has on hand. It is relatively easy for the organization to persuade itself that those tasks that it is fitted to perform are worth doing. Let us point out that although this interpretation of the Bureau's interest in marihuana is even more speculative than Becker's, it is quite consistent with what is widely known of organizations.

In any event, taking the *interest* of the Narcotics Bureau in marihuana legislation as given, Becker proceeds to describe in some detail the Bureau's entrepreneurial efforts. These included the diligent promotion of an image of marihuana use as vicious, debilitating, and a major threat to the general welfare. This promotion entailed the use of the Bureau's already considerable prestige as an authority in the field of drugs, and the dissemination, under its own name and through persons and organizations to whom it freely provided prepared materials, of its message to the mass media. This *publicity* effort led to five days of hearings by the Congressional committee that was considering the aforementioned anti-marihuana bill. Having prepared the bill, the Bureau was of course the principal witness at these hearings ("reefer" smokers sent no delegation). The only potentially troublesome obstacles to passage of the bill were the objections of the hemp-seed oil and birdseed industries, who feared that their business operations might be hampered by the proposed legislation, and these were neutralized by minor changes in the bill, which swiftly became law.

Sorokin and Becker represent two strikingly different approaches to the sociology of law. Sorokin emphasizes the logical connection between the laws and the dominant values of the culture; for him, the men who make the laws become, so to speak, the instruments through which the culture mentality spells out its implications in specific legal rules. In contrast to this interpretation the illustration from Becker emphasizes the tenuousness of the connection between the laws and the cultural values. For him, the men who make the laws are men with their own axes to grind; by virtue of their determination, their organization, their access to the instruments of publicity and political power, they "sell" their version of public morality to the custodians of the legislative machinery.

Perhaps these two approaches are not as irreconcilable as they may seem. Sorokin is concerned with the *general character* of the body of laws that prevail at a given time, and how this character changes from time to time. It may be that valid generalizations are possible on this level, without requiring that every single

35

law bear the stamp of that character to the same degree. Becker is interested in the process whereby *particular* laws are hammered out, but even Becker points out that one element in this process is persuading the relevant publics that the proposed law is instrumental to widely accepted values. Furthermore, it may be that the implications of widely held values for specific areas of conduct may be highly variable. In some areas they may be relatively clear and unequivocal, leaving little room for casuistry and contending interpretations; in some they may be obscure and uncertain, so that much depends on the powers of persuasion and the political influence of groups with variant interests.

Deviance and Other Disvalued Roles

Whereas deviant roles are socially disvalued roles (that is, they are typically low-status, undesirable roles), not all disvalued roles are deviant— despite the tendency to stretch the term "deviant" to cover everything that is disvalued. For example, the roles of slave, hunchback, moron, sick person, and the blind are disvalued, but socially they are felt to be different from such roles as coward, thief, scab, or adulterer. What the latter have in common is the notion of a person who knows what he is doing and is capable of doing otherwise, but who *chooses* to violate some normative rule, and so may legitimately be held to account for his behavior. By way of contrast, no one in his right mind chooses to be a moron, the social meaning of which is "one who is deficient in intelligence." We see, then, that there are disvalued roles that are "unfortunate" but not "reprehensible." It should be noted that Erving Goffman [16] has written most brilliantly on stigma, the taint that attaches to those who occupy disvalued roles. He has analyzed at length the effects of stigma upon self-conceptions, and the tortuous maneuvering of the stigmatized in an effort to maintain self-respect and a reputable public image. But, more relative to the point at hand, he has also emphasized the importance of not confounding deviance with being disvalued, which it shares with other, not necessarily deviant, categories.[17]

We have seen how certain kinds of acts may, over time, migrate (so to speak) from one deviant category to another. What was once a "sin" or a "vice," for example, may be elevated to the gravity of a "crime," or reduced to mere "bad taste"—and in like fashion the sinner may become either a "criminal" or a "boor." Acts may also migrate from deviant to non-deviant but disvalued categories, or in the reverse direction. Or they may move out of the realm of the disvalued altogether, into that of the neutral or the positively valued. We are not suggesting that any act may freely move into any category or, that cultures are completely arbitrary about this. On the contrary, what we are speaking of now is precisely the task of investigating the ways in which they are *not* arbitrary, in which the social structure and the cultural context determine this movement.

The role of the sick person is of special interest in this regard, because so much behavior that was once regarded as vicious, depraved, or criminal is now widely regarded as a manifestation or symptom of an illness. Indeed, this trend is one of the major cultural movements of the past 50 years or so, but it has been only meagerly documented and its determinants scarcely investigated.[18]

Homosexuality in certain of its forms—e.g., between an older man and a youth —has been positively valued in some cultures, as in ancient Greece. In Christian countries it has generally been regarded as a vice. In many quarters today, however, the homosexual is regarded as a sick person, although homosexuality is conceded

[16] Erving Goffman, *Stigma: Notes on the Management of Spoiled Identity* (Englewood Cliffs, N.J.: Prentice-Hall, 1963), *passim.*
[17] *Ibid.,* Chap. 5.
[18] See Barbara Wooton, "Sickness or Sin," *The Twentieth Century* (1956), 159:432–442.

to be an obscure sickness and peculiarly difficult to treat, possibly "incurable." The Wolfenden Report, prepared for the British Parliament, clearly stated what is at issue:

> There are two important practical consequences which are often thought to follow from regarding homosexuality as an illness. The first is that those in whom the condition exists are sick persons and therefore should be regarded as medical problems and consequently primarily as a medical responsibility. The second is that sickness implies irresponsibility, or at least diminished responsibility.[19]

The Report concluded, it may be noted, that homosexuality is not a disease. On the other hand, it also recommended that "homosexual behavior between consenting adults in private should no longer be a criminal offense." [20] This recommendation was not based on the view that homosexuality is morally acceptable, but primarily on the grounds that the public interest would not be served by subjecting it to criminal sanctions. It must be added that there are also those who regard homosexuality as neither sin, vice, nor sickness, but just "the way some people are" and essentially a private matter.

In like manner, masturbation, once an abominable sin, is now widely regarded as a medical problem, and then only if "excessive;" drug users are less likely to be abhorred as "dope fiends" and more likely to be pitied as sick people; heavy drinkers are less likely to be regarded as devotees of a vice and more likely to be regarded as the victims of a disease; and there is a growing tendency to think of the "bad child" as not really bad but sick or "emotionally disturbed." (We have been much slower to reconsign the misbehaving adult from a deviant role to the sick role.)

The tendency to think in terms of sickness rather than wickedness and vice is generally regarded as more kindly, compassionate, and humanitarian. However, it should be noted that the sick role, especially if the sickness is "mental," is also a disvalued role, and not accepted complacently. There are many people who would rather be regarded as bad or morally imperfect than as mentally ill. Becker [21] cites the example of psychiatrically indoctrinated individuals who, in order to reconcile themselves to the regular use of marihuana, must neutralize the tendency to think of themselves as neurotic or mentally ill.

Although we are dealing with a very general trend in our society, the predominant view, in each of our illustrative cases, is that the behavior in question is deviant. However, in no case is there consensus, and the same individuals are often uncertain and variable in their attitudes. This uncertainty and variability are reflected in public controversy over ambiguities in the social definition of—for example—the homosexual, the drug user, the drinker, and the misbehaving child; and in changing and conflicting procedures for dealing with the same kind of behavior, and even the same individual.

Social Control

Our survey of the scope of the field concludes with ways of dealing with the question: "Why do men *not* misbehave? Why do most people do what they are expected to do without even considering deviant alternatives, or teeter on the edge of deviance and then step back? Having broken a rule once or twice—or a hundred times—why do they stop? Or, if we think in terms of social definitions of the self, how do men become redefined from deviant characters to

[19] *The Wolfenden Report: Report of the Committee on Homosexual Offenses and Prostitution* (New York: Lancer Books, 1964), p. 30.
[20] *Ibid.*, p. 53.
[21] Becker, *Outsiders: Studies in the Sociology of Deviance*, pp. 76–77.

conforming characters, or—what is not quite the same thing—to *former* deviants (*e.g.*, "ex-drunks," "ex-criminals," "ex-addicts," "reformed sinners")? As we observed on the very first page of this book, we cannot answer these questions without answering the question, "How do we explain deviance?" Certainly every theory about what produces deviance has implications for social control—that is, the prevention and unmaking of deviance. Still, all our answers to questions about social control do not follow obviously from answers to questions about the *causes* of deviance.

Although deviance is not illness, we may draw certain analogies between the two. First, we may know a great deal about what causes a certain disease, and yet have but limited knowledge about how the disease process may be halted or reversed, either by the body's spontaneous mechanisms of defense—the *vis medicatrix naturae*—or by deliberate medical intervention. By the same token, even though we may have attained considerable knowledge about how people arrive at deviance, and although such knowledge is our most valuable single resource in constructing a theory of control, it need not necessarily answer all our questions about restoration to conformity, either by "spontaneous recovery" or by deliberate intervention.

Second, a thorough knowledge about the determinants of a disease always involves a number of factors. If one wants to "do something" about the disease, this knowledge suggests a number of different possible points of intervention. Should we, for example, concentrate on building up resistance or immunity, on treatment of the sick, on educating the public in how to avoid exposure, on compulsory segregation of carriers until they are deemed safe, on massive campaigns to eliminate the agent? Such decisions depend upon our command of the necessary techniques and on their respective costs, all of which involves a complex balancing of social values. By the same token, if we assume that we know all about the causation of some form of deviance, we can be confident that this knowledge will point to *combinations* of variables—some having to do, perhaps, with characteristics of the offender; some with characteristics of persons and objects in the situation; some with the nature of the interaction between them; and still others with structural features of the larger social setting—the community or even the total society—which determine the characteristics of the offender, the situation, and the interaction. Again, if one is interested in action, in doing something about deviance, questions may and do arise about where to intervene, and how. These questions in turn raise questions about *technique*—"How, in fact, can we control the variables (if indeed they *are* subject to deliberate control)?"—and *values*—"Are we willing to pay the price, in terms of resources, undesirable side effects, and restrictions on human freedom, entailed in intervening at this point or that?" If, for example, it were perfectly clear that drug addiction could be drastically reduced (1) by eliminating the sources of supply, (2) by ruthlessly hunting down all addicts and either exterminating them or permanently segregating them, or (3) by subjecting all addicts to a lengthy and compulsory course of medical and psychiatric treatment, we would still need to know by what kinds of technology and social organization these objectives could be realized, if at all, and the human costs of each of these approaches; and we would still have to obtain a working consensus, among those who determine policy, on which of these or which combination of these is worth the price.

Third, the discovery of effective treatments and cures usually depends on increased understanding of the causes of disease. We say "usually" because scientific medicine does not *always* wait upon certain knowledge of causes before experimenting with remedies. Indeed, thoroughly effective treatments sometimes long precede understanding; many proven techniques are in widespread use even

the scope of the field: II

though we haven't the foggiest idea of why they work. In a similar vein, although major steps in the direction of effective control of deviance are most likely to follow major advances in the understanding of it, even without benefit of such understanding, people still take steps of their own to control deviance. Sometimes they meet with surprising amounts of success.

In general, the results of attempts to control deviance are seldom obvious. As in medicine, the evaluation of results is often difficult, and requires refined methods and complex skills. What, for example, is the net effect on rates of juvenile delinquency of boys' clubs, the increased use of probation or parole, increased severity of punishment, detached work (the assignment of adult leaders to work with street corner gangs in their "natural habitats"), or the addition of psychiatric facilities to juvenile courts? It is difficult enough, as we have already seen, just to determine true rates, and changes in rates, of crime and delinquency. And even if we can establish what happens to these rates, there is then the problem of determining to what extent the changes, if any, can be attributed to the use of a particular technique of control.

We can be sure that rates respond to many things acting concurrently. If, following the introduction of a new technique, or the more extensive use of some established technique, rates decline, how do we know that they are not declining in response to some other change going on in the community? If rates increase, how de we know that they might not have increased more in the absence of the new method? What is most likely is that every method has different effects in different community settings, on different categories of offenders or potential offenders, and when used in different combinations with other methods. The evaluation of techniques of control, whether they are based on a theory of causation or not, is a task for which training in the methods of social science is essential. Increasingly, in fact, local, state, and national governments and private foundations are investing in controlled experimentation with various methods of control and scientific evaluation of results. "Action research" has come to signify the growing practice of assigning to action programs research arms whose function is to measure outcomes, to determine to what extent they may be attributed to the action program, and to analyze the program and results for what light they may shed on questions of causation.

Whether people in society think of them in this way or not, we have been using the expression "social control" to refer to social processes and structures tending to prevent or reduce deviance. The expression is also used to refer to any-thing that people do that is *socially defined* as "doing something about deviance," whatever that "something" is: prevention, deterrence, reform, vengeance, justice, reparation, compensation, the moral enhancement of the victim (*e.g.*, by "turning the other cheek"). Cultural understandings not only define deviant behavior; they also define appropriate responses to deviant behavior. They lay down specific role prescriptions and provide a vocabulary in terms of which people may describe and justify their behavior as "doing something about deviance." We shall refer to the social organization and practices that are couched and legitimized in these terms as "the culturally organized structure of control," or, more elliptically, as "the manifest control structure," to distinguish it from the aspects of society that are relevant to the reduction or prevention of deviance but are not part of this manifest control structure.

For example, the way in which opportunities for employment are distributed, or the content of the mass media, may have important consequences for actual rates of deviance, but there may be no social awareness of these consequences, and no conscious manipulation of them in the name of "doing something about deviance." However, as such awareness develops, they may come

39

under cultural regulation and be incorporated into the culturally organized structure of control. An example is the increasing awareness, in recent years, of the possibility of deliberately organizing access to employment opportunities with a view to reducing delinquency and crime, and a number of programs have been set up—most notably "Mobilization for Youth" in New York City—with this as one of their conscious objectives and explicit justifications. In principle, any aspect of society may have consequences for the control of deviance that are not socially visible and brought under regulation. We may think of these aspects of society as the "latent control structure," always capable, however, of being incorporated into the "manifest control structure."

The manifest control structure includes a division of labor for social control. This includes the assignment of rights and duties with respect to "doing something about deviance" to "functionally diffuse" roles—i.e., roles whose control functions are included among and perhaps incidental to a variety of other functions. Such are roles of parents, older siblings, friends, neighbors, ministers, and others. In some of the simpler societies practically all the activities of social control are assigned to and performed by persons in such roles. In the more complex societies, however, the division of labor includes numerous roles and organizations specialized for various control functions. The specializations, in turn, may be broad or narrow. They may include prevention, detection, taking into custody, determination of guilt, diagnosis and evaluation, treatment, punishment, restitution, and so on. Such more or less "functionally specific" control agents and agencies are truant officers, police, courts, correctional institutions, inspectors, auditors, now and then deans of men, and certain social agencies and youth-serving organizations. These in turn may be organized into a complex network through which deviants and potential and suspected deviants may be transported, as it were, varying distances and along various routes, in the course of which they undergo "processing" of various kinds.[22]

The study of the manifest control structure includes the study of the organization of this network of agents and agencies, the organization of the units or "stations" on this network, and the ways in which practice is shaped by the culture and the organization. Thus there is a growing literature on the social organization of correctional institutions and how their capabilities and functioning depend on their internal structure and their relationships to their environments.[23]

Finally, since responses to deviance are themselves subject to normative regulation, and since normative regulation implies the possibility and indeed the likelihood of deviance, the manifest control structure itself becomes a major locus of deviance. The culture places in the hands of parents, police, judges, foremen, inspectors, staffs of correctional institutions, and others, great responsibilities and also great power. Whatever processes are at work producing deviance in the general population are also at work among the occupants of these roles, among whom deviance may take the form of negligence, favoritism, cruelty, corruption. Thus we have traveled full circle and are confronted with the problem of the social control of the agencies of control. Quis custodiet ipsos custodes? Who will guard the guardians?

22 This conception of the control structure as a "flow chart" is elaborated in Albert K. Cohen and James F. Short, Jr., "Juvenile Delinquency," in Robert K. Merton and Robert Nisbet (eds.), Contemporary Social Problems (New York and Burlingame: Harcourt, Brace, 1961), Chap. 2, pp. 112–126.
23 See, for example, Donald Clemmer, The Prison Community (New York: Holt, Rinehart, and Winston, 1958); Donald Cressey (ed.), The Prison: Studies in Institutional Organization and Change (New York: Holt, Rinehart, and Winston, 1961); Gresham M. Sykes, The Society of Captives (Princeton: Princeton University Press, 1958).

levels
and types
of theory

four

Since there are as many ways of misbehaving as of behaving, and since every way of misbehaving has been explained in many ways, we feel that there is little sense in attempting here an encyclopedic inventory of explanations. We also feel that it would be fruitless to try to set forth a rigid classification scheme by which each theory of behavior would fall under only one category: due to the fact that most theories contain a number of elements, each theory, though like some others in certain respects, is unlike them in other respects—and therefore, any attempt to lump together several under a single heading is bound to distort and falsify. The following scheme is, therefore, to be regarded as one way of characterizing differences in *emphases* among actual theories. It will be useful in comparing and contrasting actual theories to be presented later.

The Psychological Level
of Explanation

All attempts to explain behavior, deviant or otherwise, involve reference to something about the actor—the structure of his personality, his perspectives, values, goals, interests, temperament, needs, drives—and something about the situation in which he acts. Any act we can think of could have turned out differently if some other person had stood in the actor's shoes, or if the situation had been in some respect different. Theories of motivation may be characterized partly by those variables or properties on the actor side which are considered relevant (*i.e.*, make a difference to the outcome), and those on the situation side which are similarly considered. However, these variables alone will

Figure 1. Research Strategies for Theories of Deviant Behavior

a. *Kinds of People and Frequencies of Deviant Behavior*

| | Behavior | |
Kinds of People	Deviant	Non-deviant
P_1		
P_2		

b. *Developmental Background and Kinds of People*

| | Kinds of People | |
Developmental Background	P_1	P_2
B_1		
B_2		

c. *Kinds of Situations and Frequencies of Deviant Behavior*

| | Behavior | |
Kinds of Situations	Deviant	Non-deviant
S_1		
S_2		

not determine the outcomes. Two theories might identify as relevant the same variables, but they may conceive the interaction that occurs when actor and situation meet—the chemistry, so to speak, of the reaction—differently, so that the outcome differs. The processes through which the variables interact and which determine the outcomes, whether these processes are located within the actor or in the conjunction of actor and situation, may be called *motivational mechanisms*.

Emphasis on the Actor

Many theories about deviant behavior assume that most of the variance—the differences in outcome—can be accounted for in terms of differences on the actor side. They assume that the question of explanation resolves, essentially, to: "What sort of person would do this sort of thing?" Insofar as the situation plays a role, it is treated as a triggering or "precipitating" circumstance, releasing a tendency that is already fully formed, and which would probably find expression sooner or later anyway. We may call such theories, in their more extreme forms, "kinds-of-people" theories. The central task of such theories is to devise a classification or typology of personalities, of which each

levels and types of theory

d. Conjunction of Persons and Situations and Frequencies of Deviant Behavior

| | Kinds of Situations | |
Kinds of People	S₁	S₂
P₁		
P₂		

e. Interaction Process and Deviant Outcomes

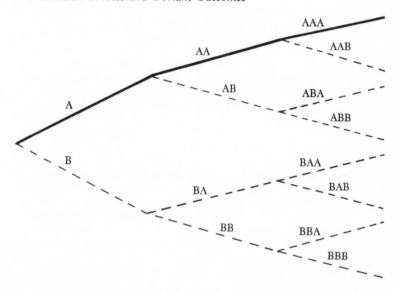

type has a propensity to certain kinds of behavior. One or more of these types may be prone to deviance in general, or to some specific type of deviance. These types may be conceived of in terms of biological characteristics, either hereditary or acquired, or in terms of purely psychological characteristics, such as personality structure, temperament, or dominant underlying needs. The research strategy usually followed by such theories is to obtain samples of the assumed types (the "independent variable") and to determine for each the presence or absence (or frequency) of deviance. This is illustrated in Fig. 1a. The test of the theory is the accuracy with which it predicts the rows in which the deviant cases will fall.

Such theories lead naturally to the question: "How did they get that way?" The problem of explanation may then be conceived of in these terms: "How do people become the kinds of people who commit deviant acts?" If the answer is not "heredity," or some pre- or post-natal biological accident, the answer takes the form of a theory of personality development or learning. The independent variable becomes some background event or circumstance, or pattern of events or circumstances, that, according to the theory, should produce such a personality. These might be, for example, attitudes and characteristics of the parents, early frustrations and deprivations, or social class background. The research strategy

43

of theories that try to relate developmental background to deviance is illustrated in Fig. 1b.

The greatest part of the literature of deviance theory is concerned with these closely related ways of stating the theoretical issue. To summarize: they assume that, for practical purposes, differences in the situation surrounding the deviant act are not very important, and the important question is: "What sorts of people commit deviant acts, and how do they get that way?"

Emphasis on the Situation

In their pure or extreme form, these theories assume that people who commit deviant acts are not special sorts of people; rather, anybody, given the appropriate circumstances, might do the same. These circumstances might be formulated in terms of provocation, temptation, example, extreme stress, opportunity. If deviance is thought of not as the commission of deviant acts but as the acquisition of a deviant character, the relevant variables on the situation side have to do with those that determine the likelihood of apprehension, identification, and selection for treatment as an offender. Sometimes, kinds-of-people theories take account of situational variables by providing, alongside the inherently deviance-prone types, for another type—the "accidental," "incidental," or "normal" criminal—who is essentially the "normal" or "average" man, responding in a *normal* way to *abnormal* situations. The research strategy for theories emphasizing the role of the situation is illustrated in Fig. 1c.

Conjunctive Theories

Theories of this sort emphasize the conjunction of both actor and situation variables in determining the deviant act. Both may vary along certain dimensions; certain combinations or "mixes" produce deviant acts. The research model is illustrated in Fig. 1d. Both rows and columns here represent the independent variables; each cell represents a conjunction; the figures in the cells are frequencies of deviant behavior. For example, the row variable may be (to use an old-fashioned expression) "strength of character" and the column variable, "opportunity." A comprehensive, general theory would also provide a rule for predicting the outcome of any particular conjunction. For example, if the column and row variables are given numerical weights, the rule might predict that the frequencies in the cells will be some function of the sum (or perhaps the product) of the two magnitudes.

Interaction Process

In conjunctive theories, deviance is the outcome of interaction between actor and situation, but the interaction is treated as a single episode. In these theories, if we are provided with certain data about the actor and certain data about the situation, the act is determined. There is, as it were, an abrupt move from a state of conformity to a state of deviance. The deviant act is like the reaction that occurs when we bring together two chemical substances. In theories that emphasize interaction *process*, the deviant act develops over time through a series of stages. Some individual, in the pursuit of some interest or goal, and taking account of the situation, makes a move, possibly in a deviant direction, possibly with no thought of deviance in mind. However, his next move—the continuation of his course of action—is not fully determined by the state of affairs at the beginning. He may, at this juncture, choose among two or more possible directions. Which it will be will depend on the state of the actor and situation at *this* point in time, and either or both may, in the meantime, have undergone change. For example, while one is deliberating about breaking

44

into a parked car, his buddy may get cold feet and "chicken out," or a policeman may just happen to turn the corner. These are now new problems and possibilities to conjure with. Certain moves are now foreclosed and others, scarcely anticipated at the outset, are now inviting or may even seem inescapable. In short, what these theories add is a conception of the act itself as a tentative, groping, feeling-out process, never fully determined by the past alone but always capable of changing its course in response to changes in the current scene.

In much simplified form, the theoretical model and research strategy, better represented by a "tree" than a table, are illustrated in Fig. 1e. Each line segment represents a move in a course of action. The completed pathway A, AA, AAA—here represented by solid lines—is the course of action that, according to the theory, culminates in deviance. The other pathways, represented by broken lines, are the other courses that action *could* have taken. Pathways are not predictable from initial states or initial acts alone; prediction is *contingent* on the state of affairs following each move. These states of affairs—the variables or combinations of variables that, according to the theory, determine the next move—are not indicated on the diagram. The diagram should be read: The initial act is A or B, depending on whether the initial state of affairs is *x* or not-*x*. If, following A, the state of affairs is *y*, then the next move is AA. If the state of affairs is not-*y*, then the next move is AB. If, following AA, the state of affairs is *z*, then the next move is the deviant outcome AAA. If the state of affairs is not-*z*, then the next is AAB. The theory may, of course, contemplate more than one pathway to deviance, or different pathways leading to different kinds of deviant actions as well as to conformity. Theories constructed on the tree model may also be used to explain or predict movement *from* deviance, one or more pathways leading to restoration to conformity, others to continued or intensified deviance. The test of interaction process theories is how well observed pathways correspond to those which the theory would predict.

We shall not attempt here to evaluate the several types of theories we have discussed. However, we should note that each of them invites attention to something that is surely relevant to a rounded, comprehensive theory of deviant behavior; and that interaction process theories come closest to making provision, somehow, for the full range of relevant considerations. However, precisely because they come closest to recognizing the full complexity of the real world, they are most difficult to formulate in neat, tight, logical, and testable systems. Perhaps the reason for the small number of serious attempts to formulate such theories is that the task is so forbidding.

The Sociological Level
of Explanation

The countless theories and fragments of theories that fall under one or another of the foregoing headings have this much in common: they are concerned with the question: How do we account for the difference in behavior between this person and that, or this person today and the same person tomorrow? Attempts to answer such questions and that seek the answers in differences among persons, in the situations they face, and in the interactions between them, we may call *psychological*. All actions are proper subjects for inquiry on the psychological level. But we may ask another sort of question as well. Actions are not only events in the biographies of individuals—things that individuals do; they are also events located somewhere in a social system or structure—in a family, a neighborhood, a city, a region, an organization, a country. Different kinds of deviant acts are variously distributed within a given social structure, and

45

these distributions differ from one time to another and from one structure to another. It also makes sense to ask: What is it about social structures—their organization, their cultures, their histories—that accounts for differences within and between them? Durkheim long ago remarked that each country, and each major region and population segment within each country, had its own characteristic suicide rate, and that these rates were remarkably stable, although over a period of time two countries, or some other units of analysis, might change their relative positions in the rank ordering of suicide rates. The suicide rate is particularly apposite because it is obvious that the same individuals are not involved in comparisons at two different times. It is clear, then, that the rate and distribution of suicide is *a property of the system*; that there is something about the society, the region, or the group that generates its characteristic suicide rate. Such regularities of pattern may be observed not only in suicide but in all sorts of deviant actions, and also in such things as birth rates, age at marriage, income distributions, gross national products, voting participation, and religiosity. In every case we are confronted with the question: What other properties of the system account for *this* property?

We may call this level of inquiry *sociological*. We do not oppose sociological explanations to psychological explanations; they are not rival answers to the same questions, but answer different questions about the same sort of behavior. However, they are obviously closely related, and not any theory on the one level is compatible with any theory on the other. Psychological theories have implications for the sociological level, and every sociological theory makes assumptions, explicitly or implicitly, about the psychological level. Durkheim himself, although he insisted as strongly as anybody on the radical distinction between the two kinds of inquiry, provides an example. One kind of suicide, which he called *suicide egoiste*, he attributed to weak social cohesion or a low degree of solidarity—a state of the networks of social relationships among the members of a system. He demonstrates, furthermore, that variations in social cohesion are related to variations in the suicide rate as predicted by his theory. However, he goes on to explain *why* variations in social cohesion should make a difference to the suicide rate, and at this point he talks about the effects of social cohesion upon the "states of mind" of the people involved.

> What is the end of suffering, above all? . . . The problem does not exist for the believer firm in his faith or the man strongly bound by ties of domestic or political society. Instinctively and unreflectively they ascribe all that they are and do, the one to his Church or his God, the living symbol of the Church, the other to his family, the third to his country or party. Even in their sufferings they see only a means of glorifying the group to which they belong and thus do homage to it. . . . But the more the believer doubts . . . so much the more does he become a mystery to himself, unable to escape the exasperating and agonizing question: to what purpose?
> . . . No proof is needed that in such a state of confusion the least cause of discouragement may easily give birth to desperate resolutions. If life is not worth the trouble of being lived, everything becomes a pretext to rid ourselves of it.[1]

Durkheim argues that the endless variety of agonies, disappointments, jealousies, and other individual "motives," throws little light on stability and change in rates of suicide.[2] In this sense, he is "anti-psychological." But it is equally clear that his own explanation of suicide as a function of the state of the social system rests upon assumptions about motivation. His speculation about

[1] Emile Durkheim, *Suicide* (Glencoe, Ill.: The Free Press, 1951), pp. 212–213.
[2] *Ibid.*, pp. 148–151.

levels and types of theory

motives, however, is distinctive in two respects. Firstly, he is concerned not with elements of motivation that are idiosyncratic, varying from individual to individual, but with those that are common to all suicides or to large classes of suicides. Secondly, he treats these elements of motivation as consequences of the state of the social system; as links in the chain of causation starting with the state of the system and terminating in the act of suicide.

In general, whatever the properties of the culture or social structure to which we attribute the pattern of deviance, these properties determine the behavior of the members of the system through their impacts upon their personalities, the situations in which they operate, the conjunctions of personality and situation, and the interaction processes between them. In other words, psychological inquiry is concerned with identifying variables and processes involved in the motivation of deviance and conformity, and with constructing exact theories about their interrelationships. Sociological theory is concerned with identifying the variables and processes in the larger social system that in turn shape those that are involved in motivation, and that determine their distribution within the system.

If we turn our attention to particular theories or to particular authors, we find that they differ not only with respect to the answers they give to the same questions, but to the range of issues, psychological and sociological, with which they are concerned. It is important to bear in mind, therefore, that when we criticize the ideas of some particular author, the criticism extends to *those ideas* and not necessarily to his entire system of thought. If one swallow does not make a summer, one dry well does not make a desert.

control theories
of deviant
motivation

five

Consider two people who want to do the same thing: one manages to do it because there is nothing to prevent him, but the other does not manage because something gets in his way—perhaps fear of punishment, perhaps a qualm of conscience. In this case, the difference in their behavior is the result of differences in the *controls*, either in the situation or internal to the personality. No general theory of human behavior can fail to make a place for the role of controls. Indeed, we shall speak now of theories of deviance that give to control the *central role* in the determination of behavior.

A control conception of human motivation is built around two sets of variables. On the one hand is the impulse side: a hostile, destructive, aggressive, acquisitive, or otherwise "antisocial" impulse. On the other is the control side: something inside the actor or in the situation of action that denies or forbids the expression of the impulse. The outcome depends on the relative strength of these two contenders: if the impulse is stronger, the outcome is deviance; if the controls are stronger, the outcome is the inhibition of deviance. On this basic theme, various theories play many different variations. Some account for deviance primarily in terms of variation on the impulse side; others in terms of variation on the control side. Such we may call "one-sided" control theories. Others emphasize the role of variability on both sides. Such we may call "two-sided" theories. Still others seem to take a control model of motivation for granted, and concentrate on the origins of the variables themselves. We are dealing, then, not with *a* theory but with *a large class* of theories.

Bio-anthropological Theories

These are the "kinds-of-people" theories *par excellence*. They do not, typically, analyze in detail the motivational processes involved in deviance, but it is clear from their descriptions that the kinds of people they are speaking of are deviant primarily because their deviant impulses are exceptionally powerful or their inner controls deficient—and more often both. Situational variables are usually recognized as somehow relevant, but are relegated to a minor role. The central task of theory is seen as that of determining the type or types of people who are disposed to deviance. These types, furthermore, are thought to be recognizable by measurable anatomical characteristics: the deviant disposition is an expression of the same biological processes, usually hereditary, that determine the shape of the body. The study of deviance from this point of view becomes "criminal anthropology," a branch of biology, and the chief tools of research become calipers, scales, and cameras.

Lombrosian Positivism

The "positive school of criminology," founded by the Italian physician Cesare Lombroso, was a reaction to the classical school, which assumed that men were, by and large, rational and endowed with free will. As such, they calculated the advantages and costs of any course of action, and freely chose that course in which the advantages outweighed the costs. Since men did not differ appreciably in these respects, the sources of variance were to be found principally in the situation, specifically in the rewards and penalties they could reasonably anticipate. The implication for social policy was that social control could be most effectively achieved by instituting punishments sufficiently swift, certain, and severe to counterbalance the expected gratification. Indeed, the classical school provides us with a prototype of a one-sided control theory of motivation in which the decisive role is played by "external" controls—*i.e.*, controls in the situation of action.

The positive school opposed a rigorous determinism to freedom of the will: having been shaped by biology or social circumstance in a certain mold, men are then moved irresistibly to act as they do. Rather than being more or less alike, they fall into a number of types, each type having a characteristic ingrained proclivity to virtue or to vice. The central task of theory is to identify the types and to discover the forces that produce them. The sense of freedom of choice is an illusion, and therefore control of deviance is not to be achieved by appealing to morality or by threats addressed to the calculating rational intellect. It is to be achieved, rather, by "individualized" measures, addressed to the peculiarities of each type and the circumstances that make it so.

The positivist position, which as we have said was first systematically formulated in the 1870's by Lombroso, was later elaborated on by Lombroso and his numerous followers, notably Enrico Ferri. On the basis of measurements of inhabitants of Italian prisons, Lombroso described the "born criminal," whose criminality and bodily structure alike were manifestations of his underlying *atavism*. By atavism he meant an outcropping of traits characteristic of a more primitive stage of the biological evolution of the race. Before his death, reminiscing on the dawn of this discovery, he recalls a post-mortem on the skull of the notorious brigand Villela:

> . . . on laying open the skull I found on the occipital part, exactly on the spot where a spine is found on the normal skull, a distinct depression which I named *median occipital fossa*, because of its situation precisely in the middle of

49

the occiput as in inferior animals, especially rodents. This depression, as in the case of animals, was correlated with the hypertrophy of the *vermis*, known in birds as the middle cerebellum.

This was not merely an idea, but a revelation. At the sight of that skull, I seemed to see all of a sudden, lighted up as a vast plain under a flaming sky, the problem of the nature of the criminal—an atavistic being who reproduces in his person the ferocious instincts of primitive humanity and the inferior animals. Thus were explained anatomically the enormous jaws, high cheek-bones, prominent superciliary arches, solitary lines in the palms, extreme size of the orbits, handle-shaped or sessile ears found in criminals, savages, and apes, insensibility to pain, extremely acute sight, tattooing, excessive idleness, love of orgies, and the irresistible craving for evil for its own sake, the desire not only to extinguish life in the victim, but to mutilate the corpse, tear its flesh, and drink its blood.[1]

This quotation gives the flavor of what is most distinctive of the Lombrosian brand of positivism. Standing alone, like a single quotation from any author, it is misleading. During the 35 years that he dominated European criminology, his position became much modified, largely in response to criticism. The continued centrality of the biological predisposition is revealed, however, even in his later writing:

> The study of the causes of crime does not lessen the fatal influence to be assigned to the organic factor, which certainly amounts to 35% and possibly even 40%; the so-called causes of crime being often only the last determinants and the great strength of congenital impulsiveness the principal cause.[2]

In the early years of this century, Lombrosian criminology took a severe critical battering, culminating in a devastating critique by Charles Goring, an Englishman and prison medical officer.[3] Goring carefully compared large samples of English prisoners with control groups of noncriminals with respect to the various attributes considered by Lombroso to be the "stigmata" of atavism and degeneracy. He concluded that there was no evidence of a distinct physical criminal type, and his work has since been accepted by most criminologists as the definitive refutation of the Italian school.

Hooton's Criminal Anthropology

However, the conviction that criminals are a biologically inferior lot, destined to criminality by defective heredity, and bearing the marks of their inferiority upon their bodies, lingers on and occasionally flickers up brightly enough to create a brief sensation. In 1939 the distinguished American anthropologist Hooton published a voluminous report on some 17,000 prisoners and free citizens, or "civilians." [4] Untold thousands of anthropometric measurements were made; criminals and civilians were broken down into groups considered comparable; and statistical differences were determined among offense groups and between criminals and civilians, Hooton concluded that different types of offenders tend also to be anthropometrically different, and that criminals as a group are morally, intellectually, morphologically, and genetically degenerate

---

[1] Cesare Lombroso, "Introduction" to Gina Lombroso Ferrero, *Criminal Man according to the Classification of Cesare Lombroso* (New York and London: Putnam, 1911), pp. xiv–xv.

[2] Cesare Lombroso, *Crime: Its Causes and Remedies* (Boston: Little, Brown, 1918, translated from French edition of 1899), p. 376.

[3] Charles Goring, *The English Convict* (London: His Majesty's Stationery Office, 1913).

[4] Ernest A. Hooton, *The American Criminal*, Vol. I (Cambridge: Harvard University Press, 1939), and a popularized version of the same, *Crime and the Man* (Cambridge: Harvard University Press, 1939).

control theories of deviant motivation

as compared to civilians. He drew the conclusion, logically enough, that the key to any really decisive attack on crime lies in eugenics, the social control of reproduction.[5]

Hooton's vogue was brief. Despite his formidable scientific paraphernalia and his undoubtably conscientious effort to observe the requirements of scientific method, his research came to grief, mostly on the shoals of dubious sampling methods. His approximately 14,000 criminals were drawn from the prisons and jails of 10 states; his 3,000-odd civilians consisted of (Nashville, Tenn.) firemen and (from Massachusetts) state militiamen, hospital out-patients, and bathers at public beaches. Where the civilian controls have been selected in this manner, the discovery of significant differences between criminals and civilians can hardly be taken as evidence of an intrinsic connection between physical type and criminality. The procedure is not very different, in principle, from comparing a sampling of female criminals with male civilians; in this case the differences between the criminals and the civilians certainly lend themselves to other plausible interpretations! No amount of precision in measurement, nor refinement in statistical comparison, can overcome the fatal defect of such imperfect controls. The problem of finding comparable controls is not, however, confined to anthropologically oriented research; it affects all social research. And it is always easier to point out defects of control groups than to correct them.

Constitutional Typologies: Sheldon

A different sort of biological theory lays less stress on the significance of specific anatomical traits and attempts rather to classify men on the basis of overall patterning or configuration of bodily structure. These patterns are assumed to be determined, for the most part, genetically, and to be correlated with (a) characteristic patterns of physiological and chemical functioning, and (b) characteristic patterns of personality and temperament that are the external expressions of the internal physiological and chemical state. Just as different breeds of dogs exhibit characteristic "packages" of build, physiology, and temperament, all rooted in the germ plasm, so do men. These temperaments are not intrinsically and specifically criminal, but some of them, especially in combination with certain environmental variables, have a special affinity for criminality or delinquency.

The best-known example of the application of such typologies to the study of deviant behavior is that of William H. Sheldon, American psychologist and physician.[6] Briefly and crudely summarized, Sheldon's typology of body types is based on the relative predominance of digestive viscera, of bone and muscle, and of neural and cutaneous tissue. The first component makes for softness and roundness; the second for hardness and rectangularity; the third for leanness and fragility. The first component is called *endomorphy*, the second *mesomorphy*, the third *ectomorphy*. The endomorph tends to be easygoing, sociable, and self-indulgent; the mesomorph restless, energetic, and insensitive; the ectomorph introspective, sensitive, and nervous. Sheldon analyzed detailed physical and biographical data on 200 boys at Boston's Hayden Goodwill Inn, a rehabilitation home for boys. He concluded that although mesomorphy did not necessarily produce delinquency, it was the constitutional background most favorable to delinquency.

Sheldon suggests a variety of ways in which body type *(somatotype)* might affect delinquency. Mainly, however, it seems to work in the following way. The mesomorph is high on drive: he is vigorous, unceasingly active, quick to

[5] *Crime and the Man*, pp. 396–397.
[6] William H. Sheldon, with the collaboration of Emil M. Hartl and Eugene McDermott, *Varieties of Delinquent Youth* (New York: Harper, 1949).

51

translate impulse into action, and bold and adventurous. At the same time he is deficient in the same inhibitions to direct action—conscience, sensitivity, and reflectiveness—that are especially characteristic of the ectomorph. Taken together, these characteristics *tend* to produce a *predatory* person, one who does and takes what he wants with little regard to others. The motivational scheme is, therefore, essentially a *control* theory: mesomorphs need not *necessarily* be delinquents and criminals; if intelligent and well situated, they may turn their predatory bents to good account by becoming successful generals, politicians, or captains of industry. At any rate, Sheldon concludes with great confidence that "whatever else may be true of the delinquency I saw in Boston, it is mainly in the germ plasm," [7] and that the only really effective solution to the problem of social control is selective breeding to weed out the socially harmful constitutional types.

We will not detail the defects of Sheldon's methodology.[8] Notwithstanding the vast array of data, including photographs of each of his 200 subjects from three angles, and the intricate and sophisticated manipulation of statistics, the logic of proof is no stronger—it is perhaps weaker—than that of Lombroso almost 80 years earlier. Indeed, his definition of delinquency as "disappointingness" is so vague as to be meaningless for scientific purposes; from the very outset, therefore, any conclusion he might draw about the causes of delinquency are destined to be worthless. His "kinds of people," measured in terms of somatotyping, are intelligible and precisely defined. However, the connection between his dependent variable—his "Index of Delinquency"—and delinquency as it is ordinarily understood is obscure.

These strictures do not apply to the more careful and responsible methods of Sheldon and Eleanor Glueck's investigation of the relationship between W. H. Sheldon's somatotypes and juvenile delinquency.[9] The Gluecks compared 500 delinquents with 500 nondelinquent controls. They compared not only the frequency of each body type among the delinquents and the nondelinquents, but also the frequency with which each of 67 personality traits and 42 sociocultural factors was associated with each of the body types within the delinquent and nondelinquent groups. They found, indeed, that significantly more of the delinquents than of the nondelinquents were predominantly mesomorphic. (Forty percent of the delinquents, however, were *not* predominantly mesomorphic.[10]) They suggest two principal mechanisms that might account for observed relationships between somatotype and delinquency.

(1) Delinquency might be "largely *direct* and uncomplicated expressions of 'original nature' in the form of excessive instinctual energy and weak or erratic inhibitory apparatus. . . ." [11] This is straightforward *control* mechanism, what the Gluecks call the mesomorph's greater "delinquency potential."

(2) It may, on the other hand, be "largely indirect, reactive, or compensatory phenomena when they occur in the naturally sensitive (ectomorphic) and obese (endomorphic) body types." [12] This is an example of a very different sort of mechanism to be discussed in Chapter 6 on the mechanisms of defense.

Three general comments are in order. First, the Gluecks, in keeping with

[7] *Ibid.*, p. 872.
[8] The most effective and thoroughgoing criticism is Edwin Sutherland's in Albert K. Cohen, Alfred R. Lindesmith, and Karl F. Schuessler (eds.), *The Sutherland Papers* (Bloomington, Indiana: Indiana University Press, 1956), pp. 279–290.
[9] Sheldon Glueck and Eleanor Glueck, *Physique and Delinquency* (New York: Harper, 1956).
[10] *Ibid.*, p. 9.
[11] *Ibid.*, p. 271.
[12] *Ibid.*

52

their generally eclectic theoretical orientation, make no such sweeping claims for inherited constitutional factors as does W. H. Sheldon, nor do they arrive at his conclusions for social control through selective breeding. They insist that there are other ways of becoming a delinquent, and they suggest that the mesomorphic constitution provides *only a delinquency potential* that is likely to be activated in an appropriate environment.

Second, their suggestion that delinquency in other-than-mesomorphs may be "reactive or compensatory" calls attention to the part that the body plays, not as a source of biological energy or inhibition, but as *an object of attention endowed with meaning.* The meaning to oneself—whether it is, for example, an object of pride or shame—depends largely on its meaning to others. Therefore, how one feels about one's body and what those feelings lead him to do are not so much a matter of biology as of socially determined attitudes. From this point of view, body type (whatever the somatotype) may indeed figure significantly in the determination of behavior. But then so may any other bodily characteristic— for instance, the shape of one's nose, the color of his skin, his defects of sight or hearing. For that matter, *any* socially visible characteristic of the person might influence his actions.

Third—and this point is closely related to the second—it may be that mesomorphs are somewhat disproportionately represented among the delinquents, not because there is something special about the temperament associated with mesomorphy, but because the street life of which delinquency is so much a part is a socially organized enterprise that rewards strength, agility, and physical toughness. If people generally gravitate toward those occupations for which they are best equipped, we might well expect the athletic mesomorphs to be more attracted to delinquency than the roly-poly mesomorphs and the skinny ecto-morphs. In brief, we would expect them to have a higher "delinquency potential" for the same reason that we would expect them to have a higher "high-school athletics potential." In both cases, "the rules of the game" confer an advantage on the mesomorph.

Bio-Anthropological Theories: Conclusion

This has been a sampling, rather than a survey, of the large body of literature attempting to link biological characteristics, visible and invisible, to deviant behavior. Endocrinological theories have attributed deviance to glandular malfunctions.[13] Studies comparing identical with nonidentical twins, in which heredity is allowed to vary and environment is presumably held constant, have purported to demonstrate that criminality may be determined by heredity. Studies of family lines, of which the Jukes and the Kallikaks are the most famous, have attempted to do the same. In general, these tracts and studies, like the researches that we have reviewed, have proved at best inconclusive.

From this history of failure, it would be incorrect to draw the conclusion that the case for biology has been refuted, or that further research along this line would be pointless. The most obvious conclusion, rather, is that no conclusions can be drawn, because so much of the research has been so shoddy. Where the methodology has been respectable by scientific standards, as in the Glueck study and some of the twin studies, the research has still not been designed in such

---

[13] Good summaries may be found in Richard R. Korn and Lloyd W. McCorkle, *Criminology and Penology* (New York: Holt, 1959), Chap. 10; Stephan Hurwitz, *Criminology* (London: Allen and Unwin, 1952, and Copenhagen: Gad Publisher, 1952), pp. 45–147; Edwin H. Sutherland and Donald R. Cressey, *Criminology* (Chicago: Lippincott, 1960), pp. 54–55, 97–116.

53

a way as to rule out interpretations of the findings very different from those of the authors.

We can be sure that men will continue to be irresistibly drawn to speculation and occasionally to research on the connection between the biological constitution and deviant behavior. Nor should this be discouraged. The human constitution, and especially the nervous system and the endocrine glands, certainly have something to do with general temperament, intelligence, energy level, sexual drive, reaction time, and other aspects of personality. It is not unreasonable to assume that these aspects of personality may in turn be related, in complex ways not now understood but conceivably understandable, to specific forms of social action. But when we remind ourselves of what we mean by deviant behavior, or more narrowly by crime and delinquency—e.g., check forging, street fighting, income tax evasion, highway speeding, drug use, rent law violations, police corruption— we must realize we are dealing with an enormous variety of behaviors as different from one another as filling prescriptions, selling used cars, and teaching algebra. The most reasonable expectation, it seems to us, is that the linkages of biology to the various forms of deviance will be as various, indirect, and remote as its linkages to the varieties of conforming behavior.

Psychodynamic Control Theories

By *psychodynamic control theories* we mean theories that consider the sources of variation in the impulse and control variables to be in the biography of the individual or in the contemporaneous situation, rather than in his biological constitution. Typically, they stand squarely in the psychoanalytical tradition—or at least share wth it the idea that the wellsprings of behavior, and especially of deviant behavior, are largely irrational, obscure energies relatively inaccessible to observation and conscious control of the actor. In this sense they, too, stand in opposition to the theories of the classical school. Psychodynamic control theories, however, seldom stand alone; usually they are interwoven with other theories of motivation, especially that of deviance as a mechanism of adjustment (this will be discussed later). However, these theories are sufficiently distinct to merit separate discussion.

Psychoanalytical Instinct Theories

We have already described, in Chapter 1, the simplest and most straightforward version of psychodynamic control theories—namely, psychoanalytical instinct theories. To recapitulate, these theories assume that all men are endowed by nature with aggressive, destructive, or other anti-social drives or instincts. The impulse side is therefore not problematical. The "kinds of people" who do and do not commit crimes are distinguished by the nature and strength of their internalized controls. The task of explanation is, in the first instance, to *identify* the defect in the control structure, and in the second to *account for it* in terms of the individual's biography.

Clear-cut statements of the psychoanalytical instinct position are numerous. However, most writers who commence with such a statement of position do not adhere to it in their explanations. In their case studies, the emphasis frequently shifts from the control side to the impulse side, and they dwell at length upon the infantile and childhood experiences that have equipped the individual with abnormally strong or otherwise deviant or perverted needs and tendencies. For example, early unsatisfied needs for nourishment, attention, or love may leave a lifelong, abiding, compulsive tendency to seize or acquire what they have been denied, or its symbolic equivalent. Or early frustrations or harsh treatment may

54

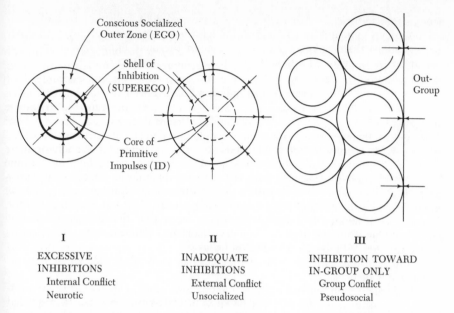

I	II	III
EXCESSIVE INHIBITIONS	INADEQUATE INHIBITIONS	INHIBITION TOWARD IN-GROUP ONLY
Internal Conflict	External Conflict	Group Conflict
Neurotic	Unsocialized	Pseudosocial

Source: Lester E. Hewitt and Richard L. Jenkins (eds.), *Fundamental Patterns of Maladjustment* (State of Illinois, no date), p. 82.

create enduring hostilities toward the world in general, or toward particular kinds of objects—say, maternal or paternal representatives; hostilities so intense that they repeatedly break through even a strong system of controls. In these, and in other ways too numerous to be reviewed here, abnormal or exaggerated deviant tendencies, only tenuously connected with or derived from a set of instincts common to mankind, may be recognized on the impulse side of the equation.

The Jenkins Typology

Psychiatrist Richard L. Jenkins has developed with exceptional clarity the logic of a control theory that is easily diagramed and purports to account for three patterns of maladjustment commonly found among children. The personality is conceived of as having a central core of primitive impulses corresponding to the Freudian id. In the normal adult or older child this is surrounded by a shell of inhibition, corresponding to the Freudian superego. Type I is an individual who has an excessive development of the shell of inhibition; he is the "overinhibited" individual who reacts to his internal conflicts by developing neurotic symptoms, such as anxiety attacks. Type II, the "unsocialized aggressive," is the opposite of Type I. He has an inadequate shell of inhibition, and gives free rein to his primitive impulses. Type III, the "socialized delinquent," has a normal shell of inhibition towards members of the in-group—*e.g.*, the gang; towards members of any out-group there is a deficit of inhibitions, and therefore free expression of the primitive impulses.[14]

Here then, parsimoniously constructed out of a few essential materials, is a typology of three kinds of people to account for three kinds of problem behavior. In the larger work from which this typology is drawn, Hewitt and Jenkins attempt to assign problem children to these types on the basis of behavioral indices, and to

[14] Paraphrased from Richard L. Jenkins, "Psychiatric Interpretations and Considerations of Treatment," in Hewitt and Jenkins (eds.), *op. cit.*, pp. 81–83.

demonstrate statistically that each type is associated with a distinct type of situational or developmental background. Although these correlations are open to other interpretations than Jenkins', the study is one of the more impressive attempts to validate statistically an essentially Freudian theory of deviance.

Types of Faulty Control Structures

1. Superego defect. Explanations in terms of controls may differ with respect to the kinds of defects of control they emphasize and how they explain them. For example, several different defects of the conscience or superego have been described. These include (a) the failure of the superego to develop at all, resulting in a person devoid of moral sense or, as he is sometimes called, a "psychopathic personality;" (b) a weak, sporadically functioning, easily neutralized superego; (c) a superego that forbids the expression of antisocial impulses against members of one's in-group, but permits their free discharge against outsiders, as in Jenkins' typology above; (d) a superego that is otherwise more or less intact, but contains gaps or "superego lacunae," that interpose no effective barrier to certain kinds of deviant impulses—*e.g.,* promiscuous sexual behavior; (e) a superego that is itself delinquent—*i.e.,* that positively condones or requires certain kinds of deviant behavior.

Each of these has given rise to a considerable amount of literature attempting to account for it in terms of specific kinds of early family experience. Superego lacunae, for example, are explained as the result of the acceptance of standards of parents who explicitly support the canons of conventional morality, but who unconsciously harbor secret wishes for certain kinds of forbidden conduct, who seek to satisfy these wishes vicariously through their children, and who somehow communicate to their children that this behavior is not really forbidden to them.[15]

The theme that runs most conspicuously through this literature is the necessity, as prerequisite to normal superego development, for the child to be able to depend on the love and support of his parent. This provides the basis for his identification with his parent, which includes the internalization of the parent's moral standards. The identification process does not occur if the dependency relationship fails to develop, or if the dependency needs of the child are not satisfied by the parent, or if they are satisfied only capriciously, according to the moods or whims of the parent rather than the conduct and misconduct of the child.[16]

A topic of continuing fascination is the "psychopathic personality." Such persons may be intelligent, charming, ingratiating, prudent, and more or less successful, or they may be dull, inept, and always in trouble. What they have in common is that if they are deterred from deviant behavior at all, it is by lack of inclination or fear of consequences. Guilt, compassion, and humane regard for others play no part in their behavior, although some psychopaths may successfully simulate these sentiments. Estimates of the number of true psychopaths vary enormously. One prison psychologist states: "Psychopaths make up the bulk of prisoners." [17] Others consider it to be a rare condition, and still others deny that it exists. In the meantime, a variety of theories have been proposed to account for this kind of person, on the assumption that he exists. The most popular view attributes it to the fail-

---

[15] See, for example, Adelaide M. Johnson and S. A. Szurek, "The Genesis of Anti-social Acting Out in Children and Adults," *Psychoanalytic Quarterly* (1952), 21:323–343, and Harris B. Peck and Virginia Bellsmith, *Treatment of the Delinquent Adolescent* (New York: Family Service Association of America, 1957), pp. 56–58.

[16] One of the most careful and systematic studies in this vein is Albert Bandura and Richard H. Walters, *Adolescent Aggression* (New York: Ronald, 1959), especially Chap. 6.

[17] Raymond Corsini, "Criminal Psychology," in Vernon C. Branham and Samuel B. Kutash (eds.), *Encyclopedia of Criminology* (New York: Philosophical Library, 1949), p. 112.

control theories of deviant motivation

ure to establish, in the first few years of life—some say in the very first year—secure, satisfying relationships with affectionate, nurturant, parental figures. If these relationships are absent during the first critical years, the damage is irreversible and the child can never develop a conscience.[18]

2. *Ego defect.* In recent years there has been increasing attention to *ego defects* of various kinds. Of the structural components of personality in the psychoanalytical tradition of thought, the ego is the most variously and loosely defined. According to Hartmann, "It is a substructure of the personality and is defined by its functions."[19] Which is to say, the ego is whatever agent or part of the personality it is that does those things that have been called "ego functions." The common element that seems to define ego functions is that they stand between the id, which is blind, urgent, and irrational; the superego, which is moralistic and critical; and external reality, which sets limits to what is possible, and determines the consequences of what we do. The ego functions mediate among these three realms. It is a kind of manager, organizer, overseer, and disciplinary agent of the personality as a whole, attempting to bring its components into harmonious relation with one another, and especially to insure that they act with proper regard for the hard facts of the real world. In particular, it chastens and restrains the impulses of the id, which, if allowed free rein, will only thwart the realization of its own aims and bring disaster upon the personality.

A "weak" ego signifies, among other things, an inability to subordinate impulses, to defer gratification, and to adhere tenaciously to a rationally planned course of action. The literature on ego functions and malfunctions has contributed importantly to the identification of the different ways in which people deal with the demands of the conscience and the "real world." What this ego is, however, and how this versatile organ does all the things that are attributed to it, is a fairly obscure subject.[20]

Frustration-Aggression Theories

These theories, stemming from the work of Freud, and most systematically elaborated by Dollard and others, state that frustration typically (or, as in some of these theories, always) produces aggression, and that aggression typically (or always) results from frustration.[21] If "frustration" and "aggression" are interpreted broadly enough, these theories can be (they have been) used to explain almost every kind of deviant behavior. The emphasis here shifts from kinds of persons with special propensities for aggression, to kinds of situations or experiences that may provoke aggression in any person. The source of frustration may lie within the personality—in one's own conscience, for example—or in the

[18] Hervey M. Cleckley, "Psychopathic States," in Silvano Arieti (ed.), *American Handbook of Psychiatry* (New York: Basic Books, 1959), Chap. 28; William McCord and Joan McCord, *Psychopathy and Delinquency* (New York: Grune and Stratton, 1956); John Bowlby, *Forty-four Juvenile Thieves* (London: Bailliere, Tindall and Cox, 1946); Loretta Bender, "Psychopathic Behavior Disorders in Children," in Edward Podolsky (ed.), *Encyclopedia of Aberrations* (New York: Philosophical Library, 1953), pp. 431–439.

[19] Heinz Hartmann, "Comments on the Psychoanalytic Theory of the Ego," in Kurt S. Eissler, *et al.* (eds.), *The Psychoanalytic Study of the Child*, Vol. V (New York: International Universities Press, 1950), p. 75.

[20] The most elaborate analysis of the role of the ego as a controlling agent is Fritz Redl and David Wineman, *The Aggressive Child* (Glencoe, Ill.: The Free Press, 1957).

[21] John Dollard, Leonard W. Doob, Neal E. Miller, O. H. Mowrer, and Robert R. Sears, *Frustration and Aggression* (New Haven: Yale University Press, 1939). See also Elton B. McNeil, "Psychology and Aggression," *The Journal of Conflict Resolution* (September 1959), 3:195–294; O. H. Mowrer, "Frustration and Aggression," in Branham and Dutash (eds.), *op. cit.*, pp. 176–186.

control theories of deviant motivation

environment. The strength of frustration depends on the strength of the needs, wishes, or impulses that are thwarted, and as the strength of frustration varies, so does the intensity of the impulse to aggression. However, the manner in which it is expressed and the object at which it is directed will depend on controls operating at the time. If the controls are strong enough to prevent the expression of aggression outwardly, it may be directed against the self. If it is directed outwardly, its object may be the source of aggression itself, though perhaps internal or external controls will deflect it toward some substitute target. It may also be rendered harmless, so to speak, by sublimation; in this case the aggressive energy is used up in some socially acceptable or constructive way. Possibly no mechanism has been used to explain so much deviant behavior as the frustration-aggression hypothesis, and it is as popular in common-sense thinking as it is in the professional literature.

Frustration-aggression theory has been cultivated mostly by psychiatrists and psychologists. Henry and Short's study on suicide and homicide is, therefore, of special interest to us because it illustrates the use of frustration-aggression theory by sociologists in an attempt to solve a sociological problem: to account for variations in rates of suicide and homicide among different social categories and through time.[22]

These authors assume that suicide and homicide are both aggressive acts resulting from frustration, the suicidal aggression directed against the self, and the homicidal against some other person. Variations in suicide and homicide among the positions or categories of a social system depend, therefore, upon (a) the intensity of frustration associated with those positions, and (b) those factors associated with those positions that determine the direction of the resultant aggression. The authors use the business cycle—fluctuations of prosperity and depression—as an index of the strength of frustration. They assume that the direction of aggression is determined by "the strength of the relational system"—that is, the degree to which the actor is constrained in his action by his relationships to others. The greater this "external constraint," the easier it is for him to blame sources external to himself for his frustration, and therefore to legitimize the expression of his aggression outwards. The less the external constraint, the greater the propensity to blame the self and to turn the aggression inwards. In other words, *homicide varies directly and suicide inversely with the strength of the relational system.*

From this theory they derive a set of predictions concerning the effects of the business cycle upon the suicide and homicide rates of various categories of the population, and test these predictions against actual data. They conclude that the data, do, in general, support their theory.

This study is as interesting as an exemplar of scientific method as it is for its theory and findings: it proceeds onward from a set of basic assumptions to a set of carefully derived hypotheses, and thence to the collection and analysis of data designed to test these hypotheses. However, this description applies equally well to a study by Gibbs and Martin, which offers a different explanation of suicide, proceeding from a very different set of assumptions.[23] We cannot evaluate the relative merits of the two theories here; this would require a careful (and therefore lengthy) comparison of their respective clarity, precision, internal logic, and predictive power.

---

[22] Andrew F. Henry and James F. Short, Jr., *Suicide and Homicide* (Glencoe, Ill.: The Free Press, 1954); "The Sociology of Suicide," in Edwin S. Shneidman and Norman L. Farberow (eds.), *Clues to Suicide* (New York: McGraw-Hill, 1957), pp. 58–69.
[23] Jack P. Gibbs and Walter T. Martin, *Status Integration and Suicide* (Eugene, Ore.: University of Oregon Books, 1964).

control theories of deviant motivation

An Appraisal
of Psychodynamic Control Theories

If not in the terminology of the control theories, then in some other language, any theory of human behavior must make room for the idea of controls. Nobody would deny that human beings are deterred from this or that course of conduct by moral considerations or by the anticipation of undesirable consequences, and that different people are differently affected by such considerations. A great deal of theorizing about deviance on the sociological level has centered on the properties and processes of systems that affect deviance by inhibiting the expression of deviant impulses.

For example: high rates of deviance in urban areas are often explained, at least in part, as being a result of dense concentrations of strangers—strangers often transient, highly mobile over a wide area and therefore relatively anonymous, uninterested in one another's conduct or misconduct, easily able to elude the scrutiny and the sanctions of those few who do know them and do care.

Then again: the high frequency of deviance in certain parts of our large cities is attributed to the fact that the people who live there are impoverished, ignorant, discouraged, preoccupied with their own survival, afflicted with a feeling of powerlessness. They are, therefore, unable to organize effectively for the containment of deviance within their own communities or to demand of the municipal authorities effective protection and law enforcement. Both these types of explanation, often called "social disorganization" theories, emphasize the social mechanisms that affect the strength of "external controls" in deviant motivation.

Still other theories focus on those aspects of social organization—e.g., the cultural homogeneity of the community, the consistency and continuity of the various agencies of socialization to which its young people are exposed, the prestige of the elders in the eyes of the young—that affect the success with which the traditional moral sentiments or "inner controls" are transmitted from one generation to another. All of these "mechanisms of social control" are surely relevant to the sociology of deviance. But this is not to argue either that a theory that emphasizes controls, whether on the sociological or the psychological level, is a rounded theory of deviance, or that one must work with one or another of the psychodynamic control theories of deviant motivation.

Seven Limitations of Control Theories

(1) By and large, the control theories take too dismal a view of conformity. The principal ingredients of motivation, according to these theories, are the impulses to deviance, and the controls that inhibit them. One commits the deviant act because he *wants* to; because it satisfies an urge, a drive, a wish. One conforms because he *ought* to or because he had *better* conform to avoid trouble. Let us agree that this is often so. However, we need not generalize to all human conduct this killjoy theory of conformity. The reader will recall the quotation from Durkheim: "No act has ever been performed as a result of duty alone; it has always been necessary for it to appear in some respect as good." Perhaps this too is an overstatement, but there is no reason to assume that deviant impulses are opposed only by stern censors and grim warnings. Not always, but probably more often than not, the "right thing to do" is also what we have learned to *want* to do, a source of satisfaction in its own right. Most people, most of the time, work rather than steal for a living, play poker or tennis by the rules, give gifts at Christmas, help a neighbor change a tire, and buy food and clothing for their children, without feeling that they have surrendered their inclination in order to appease their conscience or avoid punishment. Neither deviance nor conformity has an

59

exclusive claim on the impulse life. We may forgo the deviant alternative in favor of conformity, not because deviance is blocked off by ego or superego controls, but simply because it does not interest us, or because it is not as attractive as the conforming alternative.

(2) The control theories also take too dismal a view of deviance. They tend to identify the deviant impulses with the egocentric, self-seeking, short-sighted, acquisitive, hostile, sensual side of the personality. However, as Blake and Davis point out, the desire or motive behind the deviant act may be socially quite acceptable; indeed, it may be a wish to conform or to fulfill an obligation.[24] The most obvious example is that of role conflict, in which the individual is caught between two incompatible role demands; he violates one, not in order to evade it, but in order to fulfill the other. Homans has emphasized that the failure of organizations to secure conformity to their norms is not necessarily a matter of the opposition of "collective interests" to "individual interests," but of the expectations of one system (for example, the work group) to that of another system (for example, the family) of which the individual is also a member.[25] Merton (see above, p. 18), in distinguishing between aberrant and nonconforming behavior, has emphasized that much deviance is principled, altruistic protest against what is felt to be an unjust order—an effort, often at great personal cost, to attack the legitimacy of a rule in the name of some "higher law." Finally, as we have pointed out (p. 7), sometimes we violate the rules of an organization, not because those rules stand in the way of private gain or satisfaction, but because they hinder the achievement of organizational goals. Thus, an officer of a military organization, a business firm, or a government department, may "stick his neck out" and violate a rule or an order for what he deems to be the good of the organization. In short, the specific goals or interests that one seeks to secure by deviant behavior may be precisely those which, in some other context, motivate conforming behavior.

(3) The control theories tend to assume not only that the motive or wish behind the deviant act is itself deviant or "bad," but also that it is closer to "original" or "unsocialized" human nature than conforming impulses. In the first place, nobody has ever been able to formulate an inventory of original or unsocialized tendencies that has commanded more than scattered and temporary agreement. In the second place, the very meaning of "original human nature," in any other sense than a range of possibilities, each of them dependent upon specific experiences for its development or maturation, has always proved exceedingly elusive and obscure. In the third place, whatever motives have at one time or another been identified with original human nature or "basic biological drives" are never exclusively associated with deviant behavior. For example sexuality, directed toward the "wrong" object or seeking expression in "inappropriate" contexts, lies behind much deviant behavior; directed toward other objects, however, and in other contexts, it supports the institutions of courtship, marriage, and hard work on behalf of others. If this sexuality is to be harnessed in the service of these social ends, it must, of course, be trained to find satisfaction in certain kinds of experiences with certain kinds of objects. Illicit sexuality, however, is not by contrast untrained. The sexual impulses that find satisfaction in fornication and adultery are no more the expression of an untamed, indiscriminate, "simon-pure" sexuality than are those that find satisfaction in marriage, and few would argue that voyeurism, exhibitionism, sexual sadism, homosexuality, and fetishism are more primitive and original than the more commonplace and conventional forms of sex activity.

(4) In all scientific theorizing there is the danger of tautology, of assuming

---

[24] Judith Blake and Kingsley Davis, "Norms, Values, and Sanctions," in Robert E. L. Faris (ed.), *Handbook of Modern Sociology* (Chicago: Rand-McNally, 1964), pp. 469–470.
[25] George C. Homans, *The Human Group* (New York: Harcourt, Brace, 1950), pp. 95–96.

60

control theories of deviant motivation

that one has discovered something that explains something else when in fact he has only given another name to that which is to be explained. The instincts, energies, or drives that represent the impulse side of the control model are sometimes such tautological inventions. For example, aggressive or acquisitive acts are often explained by underlying aggressive or acquisitive impulses. The evidence for these impulses, the grounds upon which they are imputed, turns out to be the aggressive or acquisitive act to be explained. This is akin to explaining fatigue by "exhaustion." We are not arguing that factors not easily accessible to observation and imputed on the basis of some sort of inference are necessarily tautological, or that explanations in control terms necessarily fall into this trap. The argument is rather that if something is used to explain something else, it must be based on evidence independent of that which is to be explained. Cautious and sophisticated control theorists take pains to avoid tautological explanation, but it is a tempting and easy error to fall into.

(5) Some of the difficulties that we have mentioned are related to the conception of personality as a vessel, itself subdivided into compartments linked up by conduits, and containing one or more fluid substances or energies exerting pressure on the container walls. (Some critics of this conception have tagged it "psychohydraulic.") The search for motivation then tends to take the form of identifying some attribute or quality of the act and interpreting it as an "expression" or "manifestation" of such a contained substance. Thus an illicit taking is seen as a manifestation of "acquisitiveness," a hurtful act as a manifestation of "aggression," a destructive act as a manifestation of "destructiveness." This kind of explanation of an act looks inward, to the properties of the container—especially the strong and the weak points in its walls—and its contents. Attempts at explanation proceeding from such assumptions about invisible and hypothetical substances are difficult to refute and difficult to prove. But they also divert attention from other possible meanings of an act, meanings that become manifest only when we consider the acts in the context of the ongoing activities in which it is embedded. We know that to eat need not (although it may) be a manifestation of hunger. Nor do we assume that a family man who labors for his weekly wage is giving expression to an acquisitive disposition, a soldier to a fund of aggression, a bulldozer operator to a destructive energy. In every case we want to know first what is going on: the socially defined enterprise or "game" in progress; the actor's role and stake in this ongoing activity; how the act in question affects the outcomes, to himself and others, of the various enterprises in which he is involved. Even control theorists typically think in these terms *when they are talking about legitimate activities*. However, when the act in question is normatively forbidden, they tend to switch to the "psychohydraulic" model of motivation. There is no reason to assume, however, that the meanings of deviant acts are any less various and less closely linked to the immediate situation and the ongoing activities than are those of conforming acts.

This is not to deny that explanation can ignore the internal dynamics of personality, or even that hydraulic analogies and metaphors are always fanciful. For example, it is difficult to dispute that a chain of events instigated by a frustrating experience may terminate in a hostile or destructive act directed against some unoffending object. Our main point is that before we speculate about the goings-on in the obscure caverns of the underworld of personality, we pay due respect to what is sometimes disparagingly referred to as "surface" phenomena: that which we can more readily observe, describe, and verify.

(6) Frustration-aggression theory has some special difficulties of its own. In its classical form, it asserts that all frustration produces aggression, and that all aggression proceeds from frustration. The truth of the first proposition is certainly not

61

self-evident. Misery, deprivation, trials and tribulations are among the most commonplace and everyday experiences of mankind, yet only occasionally do they precipitate manifest aggression. To sustain the theory, it becomes necessary to narrow the meaning of frustration in such a way that only those seemingly frustrating experiences that eventuate in aggression are included; or to expand the meaning of aggression so that seemingly unaggressive acts are included. As to the second proposition, there are many seemingly aggressive acts that are not manifestly linked to frustrating experiences. To sustain the theory, it becomes necessary to narrow the meaning of aggression so that only those seemingly aggressive acts that can be linked to frustrating experiences are included, or to expand the meaning of frustration so that seemingly non-frustrating experiences are included. Needless to say, these efforts to sustain the generality of the theory often lead to refined and tortured exercises in definition that are difficult to defend. There is enough evidence in favor of the frustration-aggression hypothesis to persuade us that things often happen in the way it describes, but there are enough intractible data to convince us that it is not tenable as a general theory.

(7) Most of the theories we have discussed are "kinds-of-people" theories, for their explanations of deviance stress, first and foremost, something special or peculiar about the personality of the offender. (This is not necessarily true, however, of frustration-aggression theory, for this theory holds that the tendency to respond to frustration with aggression is generically human, and does not presuppose any special type of personality.)

Kinds-of-people theories—and these are not limited to control theories—must all contend with certain difficulties. One is that most people who commit deviant acts are not continuously and unremittingly deviant. For example, most students who cheat and even most children who steal do so only on occasion and behave "normally" most of the time. To explain why *this* person commits *this* deviant act at *this* time, it is therefore necessary to go beyond the purview of control theory and require borrowings from other types of theory.

Another deficiency of "kinds-of-people" theories is that they overlook the frequency with which deviant behavior presupposes personalities that are essentially "normal"—that is, that are not distinguished by marked disorders of the impulse life or of the ego or superego. Again, we ask the reader to consider what is comprehended by the word "deviance." It includes crimes and other rule violations committed by corporation officials, judges, police officers, bank employees, lawyers, physicians, postmen, politicians, and public servants of all kinds. Some of these are humble, others exalted, positions, but they all have in common that, in order to attain and to hold them, one must ordinarily have built up a reputation for reasonable decency, trustworthiness, loyalty, self-control, and the like. Indeed, as Sutherland has pointed out in his studies of white-collar crime, some of the most notorious offenders are pillars of their communities, exemplars of civic virtue, and well-organized and disciplined personalities. In some cases, their positions may be regarded as rewards for the virtues that are the polar opposites of the defects stressed by the control theories we have examined. We are not arguing that there may not be more to their personalities than meets the eye—there always is!—or that what is distinctive in their personalities is irrelevant to an understanding of their deviant behavior. We are arguing rather that, in order to commit deviant acts, one must often first have the opportunities that go with occupying a certain social position; that, in order to occupy such positions, one must have at least the reputation for the qualities of personality that, according to the control theories, insulate one from deviance; and that, although these reputations, like the reputations of all men, are imperfect portraits of their subjects, they are usually hard-earned and not without foundation.

62

deviant behavior
as mechanisms
of defense

six

In the theories to which we now turn, there is some aspect of the deviant act that cannot be understood as simply a deviant impulse breaking through the controls. According to these theories, some impulse or wish, which may or may not be deviant according to current social norms, runs counter to the conscience or some other internal demands of the personality. Whether expressed or contained, it gives rise to anxiety or guilt. The deviant act is *a device contrived by the personality to protect itself from this anxiety or guilt*. Such devices are variously called *psychodynamic mechanisms, mechanisms of adjustment,* or *mechanisms of defense*. They do their work mostly by concealing from the actor his unacceptable wish. Therefore the actor does not know and resists exposure of the "true meaning" or function of the act. If he knew why he did it, he would again stand face-to-face with his unacceptable wish. It requires the skilled analytic techniques of the trained psychiatrist or psychologist to bring its "true meaning" to light. These mechanisms come largely from psychoanalytic theory, but many explanations of deviant behavior in these terms make little use of the other paraphernalia of psychoanalytic theory. Indeed, they have become so widely assimilated into modern thinking that very few of us fail to make use of them in explaining the behavior of our friends, our associates, and especially our enemies.

Some Examples of Defense Mechanisms

The mechanism of *displacement* or *substitution* allows some expression to the unacceptable wish, but neutralizes the anxiety or guilt that would otherwise result by substituting for the target or even the form of the act some other target or form that, on an unconscious level, means the same thing to

63

the actor. Displacement may be an adjunct to the frustration-aggression theories discussed in the previous chapter, but it includes an added element: a transformation of some aspect of the act in order to deceive its author.

Deviance is often explained in terms of *unconsciously intended side-effects*. According to such explanations, the actor's behavior is governed by a certain intent, but one that he cannot admit to himself. Therefore, he organizes his behavior in such a way that it will produce the effect intended, but seemingly as an unintended or even undesired by-product of an act with an entirely different intent. So, for example, the grief or shame felt by the parent of a delinquent child, and sorrowfully repented by the apparently contrite offender, may actually be the key to his motivation.

A special case of the unconsciously intended side-effect is *the unconscious need for punishment*: the unconscious intention is to invite punishment and thereby alleviate guilt resulting from some prior behavior or, more often, from a forbidden wish. The act chosen need bear no relationship to the censured wish. In fact, the absence of such a relationship makes it possible to experience the relief of expiation without facing the real source of one's guilt.

Reaction-formation is a technique of denying an unacceptable element of the personality through behavior that seems to affirm the opposite. For example, intense heterosexual behavior in men is often interpreted as a reaction-formation against unconscious or latent homosexual tendencies; or a truculent independence and contempt for authority is interpeted as a reaction-formation against secret passive-dependent yearnings.

Psychodynamic Mechanisms
and Conforming Behavior

These mechanisms are not exclusively associated with explanations of deviant or psychopathological behavior. They have also been used to account for behavior that is considered quite normal, or at least socially acceptable. For example, various forms of goodness may be construed as reaction-formations against nastiness: kindness against unconscious sadistic impulses, generosity against stinginess, love against hate, sportsmanship against envy. Ordinarily, however, we do not interpret socially acceptable behavior in these terms. We are most prone to such explanations in everyday life when, for one reason or another, we wish to disparage a person. To attribute his behavior to the operation of a psychodynamic mechanism is to imply that it is not the free and spontaneous expression of goodness of heart; that it does not mean what it seems to mean; that there is something "compulsive" about it; that it is slightly "sick."

The mechanisms have also been used to explain reactions to deviant behavior, especially the "need to punish." If we assume that there is within each of us a cauldron of aggressive and destructive urges, repressed and contained by a diligent ego and a powerful superego, then the criminal is doing what all of us secretly wish to do. We identify with him; vicariously we share in the gratifications of the criminal act. But this in turn stirs up guilt and threatens to loose into consciousness the wicked impulses that have been so laboriously repressed. This is a situation tailored for reaction-formation. We turn on the criminal and demand that he be punished, and by demanding punishment we demonstrate that we are enemies of evil; we affirm our commitment to goodness; we deny our own repressed impulses. Paradoxically, punishment at the same time permits expression to those very impulses. Our own aggressiveness, in the guise of justice and deterrence, is displaced upon the criminal. The aggressiveness is there before the crime is; the crime conveniently provides the occasion and the object for its release, and the

64

language and the machinery of justice in turn provide the disguise which enable it to slip by the superego unrecognized. Again, it is clear that this explanation does not only explain; it disparages punishment and stains it with the taint of psychopathology.[1]

Psychodynamic Mechanisms
in Sociological Explanations

Many sociologists are critical of explanations that make use of psychodynamic mechanisms, on the grounds that such explanations are "too psychological." Certainly they are vulnerable to criticism, but not because they are too psychological. Psychodynamic mechanisms have to do with the motivation of behavior. Sociologists—or people who are asking sociological questions, whatever they call themselves—are no less interested in motivation than are psychologists, but they are interested in it from a special point of view: how the culture and the organization of the social system help to determine the ingredients and the processes of motivation, and the distribution of different kinds of motivation within and between social systems.

An Illustration: Cohen

In my own work, I have addressed the question: Why is delinquency disproportionately frequent among lower-class youth, and why does so much of it have no manifest point or utility, but seem rather to proceed from a spirit of pure meanness, negativism, contrariness, and the like?[2] Very briefly summarized, my argument states that young people's self-feelings depend very largely upon how they are judged by others. In this country the stages on which they perform and the situations in which they are judged—most notably, the school situation—are largely dominated by middle-class people, and the standards or measuring rods by which they are judged are those current among middle-class people. They are not, however, exclusively middle-class standards. They express the dominant American value system; they pervade the mass media; and they are also applied, although in a less throughgoing way, by "respectable" working-class people. These standards include such criteria as verbal fluency, academic intelligence, high levels of aspiration, drives for achievement, capacity for sustained effort in the service of long-run goals, the ability to delay gratification, neatness, cleanliness, polished manners, and others. It is also a characteristic of American culture generally—an aspect of its "democratic" ethos—that young people of different origins and backgrounds tend to be judged by the same standards, so that young people of different social class, race, and ethnicity find themselves competing with one another for status and approval under the same set of rules. However, they are not all equally well-equipped for success in this status game. In particular, different patterns of socialization are associated with the different social classes, and middle-class socialization is far more effective in training children for such success than is lower-class socialization. For this and other reasons, lower-class children are more likely to experience failure and humiliation. In brief, they are caught up in a game in which others are typically the winners and they are the losers and the also-rans.

One way they can deal with this problem is to repudiate and withdraw from the game, to refuse to recognize the rules as having any application to them, and

[1] For an excellent statement of this theory of punishment see Franz Alexander and Hugo Staub, *The Criminal, the Judge and the Public* (Glencoe, Ill.: The Free Press, 1956), pp. 214–223.

[2] Albert K. Cohen, *Delinquent Boys: The Culture of the Gang,* (Glencoe, Ill.: The Free Press, 1955).

deviant behavior as mechanisms of defense

to set up new games with their own rules or criteria of status—rules by which they *can* perform satisfactorily. It is not, however, quite that simple. The dominant value system is also, to a degree, *their* value system. They have, to a certain extent, internalized its rules also. They can *tell* themselves that they don't really care about what people think of them, and about the things these people think are important, but their internalized values, even if repressed, threaten always to break through and dilute their satisfaction with the alternative they have chosen. Therefore, to buttress this choice, to protect it from incursions from "the enemy within as well as the enemy without," they resort to reaction-formation. They not only reject the dominant value system, but do so with a vengeance. They "stand it on its head"; they exalt its opposition; they engage in malicious, spiteful, "ornery" behavior of all sorts to demonstrate not only to others, but to themselves as well, their contempt for the game they have rejected.

This theory has been severely mauled by its critics, and can no longer stand without modification. However, we are not at the moment concerned with its validity. We are interested in it as an example of the explicit utilization of the mechanism of reaction-formation in a theory designed to answer a sociological question. The aforementioned *Delinquent Boys* is concerned with the way in which the organization of the social system produces the ambivalence to which the reaction-formation is a solution.

An Illustration: Chein and Rosenfeld

These authors, psychologists who have done extensive research on narcotics use in New York City, have been concerned both with the personality characteristics of narcotics users and the social distribution of narcotics use by age, class, ethnicity, and locality.[3] They conclude from their data that all juvenile drug addicts are severely disturbed individuals: "In terms of personality structure, one may say that the potential addict suffers from a weak ego, an inadequately functioning superego, and inadequate masculine identification."[4]

Our interest at the moment, however, is focused on the relationship between age and narcotics addiction. Chein and Rosenfeld note that the age of 16 is one of exceptionally high susceptibility to involvement in drug use. They note also that this is the age which in our society is often perceived as a steppingstone toward adulthood.

> We know also that the spread of drug use in delinquent gangs tends to be associated with the breakup of the gang at a time when some of the healthier members begin to be concerned with the pleasures and responsibilities of adulthood. Until then, the activities of the gang—rumbles, fights, hell-raising, competitive sports—offer to members and hangers-on a measure of shared status, of security, and of a sense of belonging. But as the group grows older, these joint activities are given up as "kid-stuff," and the maturing youngsters develop more individual concerns about work, future, and a "steady" girl. It is at this stage that those members or hangers-on who are too disturbed emotionally to face the future as adults find themselves seemingly abandoned by their old cronies and begin to feel increasingly anxious.[5]

It is at this stage that the addiction-prone youngster, who may in the past have dallied with drugs, but not in a serious way, turns increasingly to them to

[3] Isidor Chein and Eva Rosenfeld, "Juvenile Narcotics Use," *Law and Contemporary Problems* (Winter 1957), 22:52–68.
[4] *Ibid.*, p. 60. For a contrary view, see Harold Finestone, "Narcotics and Criminality," *Law and Contemporary Problems* (Winter 1957), 22:69–85.
[5] Chein and Rosenfeld, *op. cit.*, p. 62.

deviant behavior as mechanisms of defense

bolster his confidence, to deaden his anxiety about his inadequacy to the demands of adulthood, and for pleasurable relief in situations of strain. The principal mechanism here may be called "escape" or "avoidance": it is a device to avoid clear confrontation with one's limitations and also to narcotize any residual guilt and anxiety. Note that the problem is not simply a function of a certain kind of personality. It arises when a certain kind of personality is confronted with certain kinds of demands—demands that arise or are intensified when the person moves from the status of "child" or "kid" to that of "man" or "adult." They are expectations that attach to social roles, and are therefore part of the culture of the surrounding social system. The problem of adjustment with which these young people cope by means of psychodynamic mechanisms is therefore structured, in part, by the nature of the social system.

An Illustration: The McCords

Few topics in deviant behavior (or emotional illness, depending on how one chooses to define it) have spawned more speculation and research than have alcoholism and problem drinking. Almost every perspective on human behavior—pastoral psychology, physiology, biochemistry, learning theory, psychoanalysis, sociology, anthropology—has been brought to bear on the subject. Among psychiatrists and clinical psychologists, and probably among students of the subject in general, the most influential views are in the psychoanalytical tradition, going back to Freud's own writings on alcoholism. Although even these views vary greatly among themselves,[6] the following three themes recur with impressive regularity.

(1) Alcoholism is associated with unusual experiences at the oral stage of development, the stage when the infant is completely dependent upon the solicitude and nurturance of the mother. During this stage, the infant's principal avenue to and instrument of contact with the world is the mouth. Since its principal gratifications and frustrations are oral, eating and drinking, biting and kissing, and all other oral activities acquire emotional meanings and overtones associated with the quality of its experiences and relationships with others, primarily its mother. The experiences during the oral stage that are held to be most significant for the development of alcoholism are cruelty, neglect, deprivation, or alternating indulgence and deprivation, although excessive indulgence—the encouragement of overdependence—is sometimes implicated, too. In any case, the result is held to be the development of a personality with profound, perhaps insatiable, needs for dependency. (The development of homosexual tendencies—also traced, as a rule, to experiences in the oral stage—is sometimes considered of equal importance, sometimes secondary to the dependency need.)

(2) Later experiences lead to the acquisition of contrary needs: needs for independence and achievement, and a need to present an image of confident heterosexuality. This leads to the repression of the dependency wishes and/or homosexual tendencies, but not to their extinction; they remain permanent sources of dissatisfaction, tension, and anxiety.

(3) Alcohol is a device for coping with these problems. It relieves guilt and anxiety. It loosens inhibitions, permitting expression of repressed wishes, and at the same time blurring perception of the real meaning of one's behavior. Above all, the consumption of alcohol is itself a symbolic re-creation of a satisfying dependency relationship:

[6] For a useful summary, see Israel Zwerling and Milton Rosenbaum, "Alcoholic Addiction and Personality," in Silvano Arieti (ed.), *American Handbook of Psychiatry* (New York: Basic Books, 1959), pp. 623–644.

The alcoholic experiences unconscious and to a certain extent conscious longings for physical warmth, pleasurable skin sensations, maternal coddling, liquid and warm feelings in his stomach which are not differentiated from long-ings for security, reassurance, self-respect, independence and, at times, omnipo-tence. . . . Alcohol gives the adult what milk gives the normal infant.[7]

We will not discuss the innumerable variations and elaborations of these theories. For the most part, the theories grow out of clinical impressions, case histories, and the psychoanalytically trained imagination. To a certain extent they are supported by evidence from statistical studies, with and without control groups. The most rigorous and definitive attempt to put these theories to a test has been by William and Joan McCord.[8] These authors studied the histories of 510 boys who had been the subjects in the late 1930's and the 1940's of the Cambridge-Somerville Youth Project. This was a study of delinquency, not alcoholism. Dur-ing the course of the Project, however, counselors worked closely with about half the subjects and compiled detailed and copious data on each one; less detailed data were recorded on the half that were not assigned counselors. In 1948 and in 1956 follow-up studies secured additional data on all the subjects, now adults. The McCords therefore, had available to them, data on 510 subjects, data gathered when these subjects were children, and not data retrospectively compiled from the recollections of adults. They also had data on the adult histories of these same subjects, including reliable indicators of alcoholism. These data were thoroughly analyzed to obtain correlations between childhood backgrounds and personality, and the subjects' later alcoholism. The variables most intensely studied were taken from a theory derived from psychoanalytical literature, and supplemented by con-siderations growing out of the authors' training as sociologists. This theory is succinctly summarized in the accompanying table.

We shall not review the data here. In general, however, correlations between childhood experiences and adult alcoholism are consistent with the model. A few of the McCords' observations are worthy of special note.

(1) The data indicate that it is not dependency *needs* as such, but depen-dency *conflict* that is strongly linked to alcoholism. For example, neither maternal affection nor maternal rejection is as strongly correlated with later alcoholism as is alternation between affection and rejection. This, presumably, should lead to intense needs accompanied by ambivalence and anxiety.

(2) The data do not support the view that repressed or latent homosexuality are linked to alcoholism.

(3) The children who later became alcoholics were more often than their controls "raised in environments in which the responsibilities of the male role were neither exemplified nor enforced," and in which they were sometimes rewarded, sometimes punished for the same thing. This, the authors believe, would be likely to produce "a confused self-image, one that would tend to break down in the face of role requirements imposed upon the average adult male in America." [9]

(4) The alcoholics tended, as children, to be aggressive, manly, hyperactive, and self-confident. In the light of their other data on these same children, the authors interpret this as a facade of masculinity, masking their confusion and anxiety.

(5) Although the authors have little data bearing directly upon the role of

---

[7] G. Lolli, quoted in Zwerling and Rosenbaum, *op. cit.*, p. 627.

[8] William McCord and Joan McCord, *Origins of Alcoholism* (Stanford: Stanford Univer-sity Press, 1960).

[9] *Ibid.*, p. 83.

68

deviant behavior as mechanisms of defense

Table 5

Model of Alcoholism

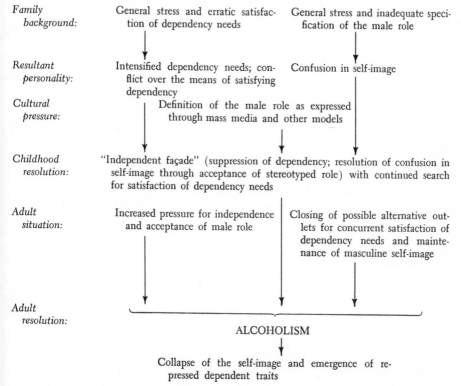

| *Family*
background: | General stress and erratic satisfac-
tion of dependency needs | General stress and inadequate speci-
fication of the male role |

Resultant — Intensified dependency needs; con- — Confusion in self-image
personality: — flict over the means of satisfying — dependency

Cultural — Definition of the male role as expressed
pressure: — through mass media and other models

Childhood — "Independent façade" (suppression of dependency; resolution of confusion in
resolution: — self-image through acceptance of stereotyped role) with continued search
for satisfaction of dependency needs

Adult — Increased pressure for independence — Closing of possible alternative out-
situation: — and acceptance of male role — lets for concurrent satisfaction of
dependency needs and mainte-
nance of masculine self-image

Adult
resolution:

ALCOHOLISM

Collapse of the self-image and emergence of repressed dependent traits

Source: Reprinted with permission from William McCord and Joan McCord, *Origins of Alcoholism* (Stanford: Stanford University Press, 1960), p. 151.

the adult situation, they speculate that this may play a decisive role in determining whether the outcome of childhood experiences will be alcoholism. Among the factors in the adult situation which they stress are: (a) the extent to which the milieu defines drinking as an enjoyable, attractive, legitimate activity; (b) the extent to which the milieu demands achievement and frustrates dependency longings, for there *are* adult situations and occupations (for example, the army) in which highly dependent relationships are socially acceptable and compatible with the male role; (c) the extent to which the adult encounters experiences in which his precarious facade of aggressive and independent masculinity is challenged, threatened, or exposed.

In short, although the McCords see alcoholism as the outcome of a certain type of childhood history, they make it clear that childhood history *alone* does not determine the outcome. It creates a type of personality that, in the face of certain kinds of adult situations, is likely to *turn to* alcoholism.

Although the McCords are more sensitive than most psychiatrists and psychologists to certain kinds of variables (for example, cultural definitions of drinking, and the extent to which the situation in adulthood indulges or denies depen-

69

dency longings), their study is not quite sociological in the fullest sense. It is addressed primarily to the question of the kinds of life histories that distinguish alcoholics from nonalcoholics. A fully sociological study might identify different positions or sectors within the same society, or even different societies; it would assign to each, on the basis of the McCords' theory, different probabilities of producing alcoholism; and it would compare these theoretically expected probabilities with the empirically observed differences in rates of alcoholism. That is, it would attempt to answer the question: How do we account for differences in the distribution of alcoholism within or among societies?

Such a step, building upon the work of the McCords, has in fact been taken in a cross-cultural study by Bacon, Barry, and Child. These authors analyzed data on 139 non-European societies, and obtained confirmation of their hypothesis:

> Amounts and patterns of alcohol consumption by adults have their antecedents partly in the degree and pattern of nurturance in infancy, the extent of demands for self-reliance and achievement in childhood, and the extent to which the expression of dependency needs is permitted in adult life.[10]

From the point of view of this book, however, this study too has an important limitation. We are interested in drinking behavior or in particular patterns of drinking behavior (for example, "drunkenness," one of the patterns covered in this study), insofar as it is *deviant*—*i.e.*, in societies or segments of societies in which it violates normative rules. This study does not consider the normative status of the behavior. If drunkenness and alcoholism in our own society were socially perfectly acceptable, they would still be worth studying, but (1) the data about these behaviors—for example, their rates and distributions—and their explanations would no doubt be somewhat different, and (2) they would not constitute problems *for the study of deviant behavior*.

An Appraisal of Psychodynamic Problem-Solving Theories

Personality and Situation

Most explanations of deviance making use of psychodynamic mechanisms strongly emphasize the importance of personality differences between deviants and nondeviants. ("Personality" is here to be understood in the sense of early-established, deeply-engrained, relatively enduring problems of adjustment and techniques of coping with these problems.) Many of these explanations lean so heavily on such personality characteristics, to the exclusion of situational factors, that they may be described as what we have already termed "kinds-of-people" theories. Our criticisms in the preceding chapter are applicable to such explanations. However, we must not apply this description carelessly. For example, some writers distinguish between deviants as those who use psychodynamic mechanisms because they are special kinds of people, and as those—not marked off in any way from ordinary people—who use them because they find themselves in exceptional circumstances. Thus M. E. Chafetz and H. W. Demone distinguish "addicted" alcoholics, who are personalities fixated at the oral stage, from "reactive" alcoholics.

[10] Margaret Bacon, Herbert Barry III, and Irvin Child, "A Cross-Cultural Study of Drinking," in Charles R. Snyder and David R. Schweitzer (eds.), *Proceedings, Research Sociologists' Conference on Alcohol Problems* (sponsored by the Committee on Drinking Behavior of the Society for the Study of Social Problems, held at Southern Illinois University, April 30 and May 1, 1964), pp. 45–47. Above quotation is from p. 46.

70

deviant behavior as mechanisms of defense

The latter have relatively healthy, integrated pre-alcoholic personalities. They use alcohol to excess when temporarily overwhelmed by external stress. . . . We believe anyone may use alcohol pathologically to alleviate anxiety, to make instinctive impulses acceptable, to strengthen defense measures, and to provide narcosis against painful reality.[11]

Many psychodynamic explanations conform to a "conjunctive" model. That is, they assume that a special kind of personality is a prerequisite to, or at least a facilitator of certain kinds of deviant behavior; but they also assume that situational factors play an indispensable part. For example, the current sitution may determine (1) whether the problem of adjustment to which the behavior is a solution materializes or reaches the necessary degree of severity; (2) whether alternative solutions to the same problems are available; and (3) whether the behavior will invite sanctions powerful enough to deter. We have seen this kind of conjunctive reasoning in the work of Chein and Rosenfeld and the McCords.

Problems of Imputation

Explanations in terms of psychodynamic mechanisms involve the imputation to the actor of the drives, wishes, tendencies, and such, that are the ingredients of his problem; of anxiety or guilt; and of some mechanism, such as substitution or reaction-formation, that gives the act a meaning different from that which it seems to have. We have already discussed, in connection with control theories, the difficulties and hazards of the imputation of such "subjective" states. If one is disposed to think in terms of psychodynamic mechanisms, he can always think of some problem of adjustment and mechanism that will make sense of any act. However, the possible things that an act *might* mean on some "deeper" level of the personality are virtually limitless; somebody else can always think of another meaning. It is not unusual for different people to defend as obvious "to the trained mind" quite different psychodynamic interpretations of the same behavior. Frequently these different interpretations are equally circular, for the only firm evidence for the underlying subjective state and processes is the behavior which they were designed to explain. Even independent evidence is difficult to evaluate, for if one digs deeply and diligently enough into somebody's dreams, fantasies, free associations, and memories, he is bound to dredge up material that can be interpreted as evidence of what he is trying to prove. Or, if we start with plausible evidence of some underlying wish or tendency, it is almost always possible to find some mechanism through which it can be reconciled with a given overt action. For example, if the overt action is manifestly consistent with the underlying wish or tendency, it can be construed as an "expression" of it. If it is not manifestly consistent with it, it can be construed as a "substitute" or "symbolic" expression. If it is the opposite of it, it can be construed as a "reaction-formation."

This is not the place for a discourse on the rules of psychological interpretation. However, we must emphasize again that these problems of imputation differ in degree of difficulty, and not in kind, from the problems of imputation in everyday life. They are methodological difficulties of a very grave order and require us to maintain an extremely critical attitude. But they are not difficulties of which the more sophisticated practitioners of psychodynamic reasoning are unaware. Much writing in a psychodynamic vein consists of irresponsible and unverifiable flights of fantasy. But much of it is cautious and sober, setting forth alternative possible interpretations, and carefully and critically marshaling evidence for and

[11] Morris E. Chafetz and Harold W. Demone, Jr., *Alcoholism and Society* (New York: Oxford University Press, 1962), pp. 20–21.

deviant behavior as mechanisms of defense

against each one before arriving at a conclusion. Even then, however, the issue may not be settled. The evidence may simply be inconclusive, or the author, with his sights aimed at the "deeper" levels of the personality, may have overlooked some much more simple and "superficial" explanation, but one nearer to the truth.

The Concept of "Unconscious"

Many writers, especially among sociologists, are critical of the very concept "unconscious," and avoid it studiously. They believe it is a mystical region, existing only in the minds of misguided psychologists, and inhabited only by convenient inventions that are born, as needed, out of nothing by spontaneous generation. This is, we think, a fair enough description of the way the concept is often used; but the truth in this criticism does not settle the question of its scientific status. If we think of "unconscious" as referring to those acts and feelings that we do not name, identify, represent to ourselves symbolically, look in the face (so to speak), and talk to ourselves about, then it seems neither strange nor mysterious nor elusive. When we scratch, we presumably itch, but sometimes we do not know we are scratching, much less itching, until somebody calls it to our attention. We were not conscious of it. Sometimes, under persistent and unremitting needling, we remain calm, and persuade ourselves that we couldn't care less—till we explode with a bang that astonishes us. We were "madder than we thought," than we were conscious of being. If we admit this much into our tent, we must consider the rest of the camel. We will have admitted that not only acts but "affect" (—that is, feelings) may be unconscious. We will not argue the point here, but we suggest that it is not a far cry to "impulses" and "tendencies."

We would also suggest that sometimes—not always, and probably not usually—we exert effort to keep things unconscious. If this is so, we will have come very close to the concept of "repression." In brief, we would argue that the problem is not whether unconscious events occur, but the grounds on which we assume the occurrence of such events. In this respect, the argument is similar to our argument about "subjective states" in general. We suspect that study would reveal that those authors who most carefully eschew the word "unconscious" will show an exceptionally high frequency of use of the word "unwitting"—which, if pressed, they would define as we have defined it: "unconscious."

We are saying that there is nothing remarkable about having, let us say, a tendency, and not being conscious of it. It may be quite another thing, however, to say that there is a tendency "in the unconscious." This expression may be defended as a figure of speech, not to be taken seriously, but it is a dangerous one. It suggests a place, a region of the mind—sort of a cave, perhaps—where sinister forces contend in darkness. Such metaphors have a way of beguiling the imagination, so that presently one finds himself constructing a geography of this mysterious place: its boundaries, its topography, its laws, its population, its principal products. This wealth of implication simply does not follow from the idea that there are things about ourselves that we take note of and indicate to ourselves, and others that we do not.

Finally, we should avoid the tacit assumption, common to much psychodynamic thinking, that since unconscious states and processes are important, that which is not unconscious is not important. To be conscious of something is not merely to give it a name and to converse with ourselves about it. It is to define it, to indicate to ourselves what is going on; and this in turn largely determines the attitude we shall take toward it, and what we shall do about it.

72

deviant behavior as mechanisms of defense

The Choice of Solution

One of the most frequent criticisms of these theories is that, even if we accept the imputation of the underlying problem of adjustment as valid, we still have to account for the choice of a deviant solution, and a particular sort of deviant solution. Different people deal with very similar problems in different ways; not the least important of these ways is to suffer, grit one's teeth, and carry on. To demonstrate the existence of a problem is not to account for these differences; something more is needed, but all too often psychodynamic explanations stop short of this something more, complacently assuming that the task is finished. This is a serious criticism, but it too must be applied selectively. Many psychodynamic theorists are extremely sophisticated about these matters, and deeply concerned about the problem of "choice of symptom." As we have seen, they sometimes insist that the behavioral outcome is not determined by the problem alone, but by differences in the situation of action. Some of them have also done important work on personality characteristics that help determine the characteristic ways in which different people deal with their problems, and the origin of those characteristics.

Even sophistication, however, is not always an adequate safeguard. If you know the actor has committed certain acts, and if you are convinced that he has a certain problem, with a little imagination you can always find something in his personality or situation that will seem to you to account for the choice of *this* act as a solution to his problem. Especially if you have a theory to defend, you are likely to overlook evidence that is not consistent with your interpretation. What is necessary is objective, standardized rules and procedures for the examination and interpretation of evidence, so that different investigators, independently following these rules and procedures, will arrive at the same conclusions.

However, all that we have said is applicable to all scientific work. Psychodynamic problem-solving theories are probably, on the whole, especially vulnerable to the hazards we have discussed, but the same kinds of questions about incomplete explanations, biased perceptions growing out of one's stake in defending a theory, and imperfectly standardized operations that make independent corroboration or disproof impossible, can be raised about a great many other theories in the field of deviant behavior.

73

introduction
to anomie theory

seven

In the two preceding chapters we have emphasized theories about the dependence of deviant behavior upon motivation and personality. We have presented sociological materials in order to illustrate the psychological assumptions underlying sociological explanations. In the remaining chapters our emphasis will be on the ways in which deviant behavior depends upon the properties and functioning of social systems. We will review a number of theories and concepts, each of which illuminates some aspect of the field of deviance, but none of which integrates their several insights into a single, coherent system.

Anomie Theory: Durkheim

The meaning of "anomie," like that of so many other sociological concepts, has undergone many changes at the hands of different authors. We will make no attempt here to review the confused history of the term, but will concentrate instead on the main line of development of anomie theory.[1] This begins with Durkheim's effort to account for "pathological" forms and consequences of the division of labor—notably for the frequent tendency of an increasing division of labor to be accompanied by imperfect coordination of the parts, the decline of social solidarity, and conflict among the social classes.[2] These

[1] For a more detailed treatment of the various meanings of "anomie," see Marshall B. Clinard (ed.), *Anomie and Deviant Behavior* (New York: The Free Press of Glencoe, 1964), especially the chapter by Clinard, "The Theoretical Implications of Anomie and Deviant Behavior," pp. 1–56.
[2] Emile Durkheim, *The Division of Labor in Society* (New York: The Free Press of Glencoe, 1964), Book 3, Chap. 1, pp. 353–373.

74

conditions occurred, according to Durkheim, when those who performed the various specialized functions in the division of labor were not in sufficiently intimate and continuous interaction with one another to permit the gradual development of a system of common rules and understandings. In the absence of such rules, unpredictability and uncertainty were magnified, the actions of people in one sector of the division of labor could not be attuned to the actions and expectations of people in other sectors, people worked at cross-purposes, and the results were confusion, inefficient performance of essential social functions, and tendencies to social disintegration. In brief, the body of common rules which is the principal mechanism for the regulation of the relationships among the elements of the social system, had broken down. This condition Durkheim called "anomie." "Normlessness" and "deregulation" come closest to capturing the spirit of Durkheim's usage.

In his treatise on suicide Durkheim distinguished three principal types of suicide, one of which was *suicide anomique*.[3] He observed that suicides increased not only in times of depression but also in times of rapidly increasing prosperity. The former seems easy to understand: peoples' customary standards of living, what they have come to expect as the rightful rewards of their labor and necessary to their status, can no longer be met. For many of them this means shame, frustration, desperation, and futility; life no longer seems worth living. But why should prosperity produce similar results?

According to Durkheim, human wants, unlike those of animals, are in principle infinitely expandable. There is no "natural" limit to what men might crave, and therefore to what might provide them a sense of satisfaction and fulfillment. The limit to men's desires, insofar as there are such limits, are set not by biology but by social rules that define, for each class of men, what it is legitimately entitled to. These rules, incorporated into the individual conscience, regulate and discipline men's aspirations, and thereby create the possibility of a sense of satisfaction and fulfillment. But the effect of "an abrupt growth of power and wealth" is precisely to upset, for many people, these customary definitions of what is a fitting distribution of rewards among the members of society.

> The limits are unknown between the possible and the impossible, what is just and what is unjust, legitimate claims and hopes and those which are immoderate. Consequently, there is no restraint upon aspirations. . . . Some particular class especially favored by the crisis is no longer resigned to its former lot, and, on the other hand, the example of its greater good fortune arouses all sorts of jealousy below and above it. . . . Nothing gives satisfaction and all this agitation is uninterruptedly maintained without appeasement. Above all, since this race for an unattainable goal can give no other pleasures but that of the race itself, if it is one, once it is interrupted the participants are left empty-handed. . . . All classes contend among themselves because no established classification any longer exists. Effort grows, just when it becomes less productive. How could the desire to live not be weakened under such conditions?[4]

Anomie Theory: Merton

Durkheim applied the concept "anomie" to the division of labor and suicide. He did not try to develop its implications for a general theory of deviant behavior. Forty-one years after the publication of the first edition of Durkheim's *Suicide*, Robert Merton published his *Social Structure and Anomie*,

[3] Emile Durkheim, *Suicide*, Chap. 5, pp. 241–276.
[4] *Ibid.*, p. 253.

a short paper of ten seminal pages, which laid the foundations for such a general theory.[5]

Merton began by making explicit a threefold distinction that was implicit in Durkheim's analysis of suicide. First, there are the *culture goals*—the wants or aspirations that men are taught by their culture. They are one aspect of the "culture structure." Second, there are the *norms* prescribing the means that men may legitimately employ in the pursuit of these goals. They are a second aspect of the culture structure. Third, there is the actual distribution of facilities and opportunities for achieving the culture goals in a manner compatible with the norms. These are the *institutionalized means*. They are an aspect of the "social structure," the objective conditions of action. It is apparent that the actual sense of frustration, despair, injustice—in general, of *strain*—does not depend on any one of these, but on the relationship among them. A "disjunction" between goals and institutionalized means can arise *either* because of an escalation of the goals *or* because of a contraction of the definition of legitimate ways of achieving them. But neither of these aspects of the culture structure needs to change for a disjunction to occur: if the actual distribution of facilities and opportunities change, as in times of depression, then conduct conforming to the norms—conduct that was once compatible with goal-attainment—no longer leads to the expected rewards.

We have identified three variables whose interaction determines the distribution of "socially structured strain." The culture structure may prescribe similar goals for all members of the system, or different goals for people in different social positions. It may prescribe certain rules for achieving these goals that are uniform for all members of society, or it may forbid to members of one position what it permits for another. No society is a perfect example of any of these extremes, but some approximate them more closely than others. For example, our own society, according to Merton, comes close to prescribing for men of all classes and conditions aspirations to "succeed," largely although not wholly in terms of monetary or material success, and the rules of the game do not differ greatly for different social positions. Other societies, notably feudal and peasant societies, subject the different orders of men to different normative restrictions on the use of means, but they also prescribe different goals for them. In all societies, the actual distribution of facilities and opportunities varies greatly among social positions, but in a different manner in each society. Of course, each of these determinants of strain may also vary over time. Merton saw our own society, with its uniformly high success goals, as one exceptionally productive, on the one hand, of effort and accomplishment, and on the other hand, of frustration and strain, especially in the lower classes with less access to institutionally permitted means.

This disjunction between goals and means, and the consequent strain, leads to a weakening of men's commitment to the culturally prescribed goals or institutionalized means—that is, to a state of anomie. Merton spells out the logically possible ways in which they can adapt to this disjunction: they may either accept or reject the cultural goals; they may either accept or reject the institutionalized means. What they do on one side is not necessarily determined by what they do on the other. We have, therefore, two variables, each of which may take two values. The logically possible outcomes are given in the following table, in which (+) signifies "acceptance," (−) signifies "rejection," and (±) signifies "rejection of prevailing values and substitution of new values."

[5] Robert K. Merton, "Social Structure and Anomie," *American Sociological Review* (October 1938), 3:672–682; revised and extended in Robert K. Merton, *Social Theory and Social Structure*, revised and enlarged edition (Glencoe, Ill.: The Free Press, 1957), Chaps. 4 and 5, pp. 131–194.

introduction to anomie theory

Table 6

A Typology of Modes of Individual Adaptation

Modes of Adaptation	Culture Goals	Institutionalized Means
Conformity	+	+
Innovation	+	—
Ritualism	—	+
Retreatism	—	—
Rebellion	±	±

Source: Robert K. Merton, *Social Theory and Social Structure*, p. 140. This table, as Dubin points out, does not quite exhaust all of the logical possibilities. See Robert Dubin, "Deviant Behavior and Social Structure," *American Sociological Review* (April 1959), 24: 147–164.

The first of these outcomes is "Conformity." The remaining outcomes are all varieties of deviant behavior. Innovators (*e.g.*, professional thieves, white-collar criminals, cheaters in examinations) adhere to the goals but reject the normatively prescribed means. Ritualists (*e.g.*, bureaucrats who slavishly follow the rules without regard for the ends for which they were designed) make a virtue of over-conformity to the institutionalized norms at the price of underconformity to the culturally prescribed goals. Retreatists (*e.g.*, tramps, chronic drunkards, and drug addicts) withdraw from "the rat race" by abandoning both goals and means. Rebels (*e.g.*, members of revolutionary movements) withdraw allegiance to a culture and social system they deem unjust and seek to reconstitute the society anew, with a new set of goals and prescriptions for attaining them. Notice that this approach to deviance focuses not on the characteristics of individuals but on the positions that individuals occupy in the social system. It is concerned with variations with respect to strain within and between systems, and it locates the sources of strain in the cultural and social structure. It is, then, a radically sociological approach. Furthermore, it makes it possible to talk about both conformity and the several varieties of deviance in terms of a simple and parsimonious conceptual scheme—*i.e.*, dichotomous (either-or) choices on each of two variables.

However, it is still a very incomplete theory. Merton does, to be sure, deal at some length with the determinants of strain and on the possible responses to strain, and he also has some observations on the determinants of the choice of this mode of adaptation or that. However, he presents no systematic classification of these determinants, much less general rules relating classes of determinants to classes of outcomes.[6] This is a significant limitation. We made essentially the same point in our appraisal of psychodynamic problem-solving theories. There we spoke of unconscious problems of adjustment, here of disjunctions between goals and institutionalized means. In either case, one possible (and perhaps the most common) response is conformity, perhaps at the cost of considerable psychic strain. As for deviant responses, there are usually several different "choices" available.

[6] Smelser has developed a theory of social movements, which also begins with the concept of strain, and then specifies a series of conditions, each one of which further narrows the range of possible outcomes, until the only possible outcome is collective behavior. This procedure might be fruitfully applied to Merton's modes of adaptation. See Neil J. Smelser, *Theory of Collective Behavior* (New York: The Free Press of Glencoe, 1963), especially Chap. 3.

77

Illustration:
Deviation in the Jewish Community
of a Small Polish Town

Rosenthal studied deviation and social change in the Jewish community of Stoczek, a small Polish town, between the two World Wars.[7] The forms of deviance included decline in religious orthodoxy, violation of the Sabbath, decrease of arranged marriages, declining attendance at Zionist organizations, and the abandonment of traditional dress. This behavior was most common among young people of the lower class. In summarizing her explanation, Rosenthal quotes the following lines from Merton:

> It is only when a system of cultural values extols, virtually above all else, certain *common* success-goals *for the population at large* while the social structure rigorously restricts or completely closes access to approved modes of reaching these goals *for a considerable part of the same population*, that deviant behavior ensues on a large scale.[8]

In Stoczek, according to Rosenthal, the success goals and the main determinants of status *for the population at large* were learning, charity, and good deeds. Although these were, indeed, pursued by all classes of people, conspicuous attainments in these respects depended upon such class-linked facilities as wealth, leisure, and family connections. In short, the lower classes were greatly restricted in their opportunities to achieve the common success goals. Hence, according to Rosenthal, the concentration of deviance in the lower class.

Rosenthal does not provide a direct answer to the question of why deviance took the variety of forms that it did. An answer is suggested, however, in her statement that "there was something in the culture which made the people in the middle and upper class have more emotional attachment to it [that culture]." [9] By implication, those who were rich in learning, charity, and good deeds placed great value on *the entire way of life* of which these were the central virtues. The Jews of the lower class, denied the opportunity to excel in the only ways in which this culture defined success, came to be less "emotionally attached" to the culture as a whole. Perhaps, to use the metaphor of the game, those who despair of ever winning, eventually not only stop trying to win, but become indifferent to or forsake the game altogether.

Illustration:
A Case from the Army

When the Japanese surrendered in World War II, I (the author of this book) was an officer in a chemical mortar battalion in the Philippines. On the morning following the news of the surrender, the battalion commander summoned me to his tent and spoke to this effect:

> This battalion has had excellent morale to this point. One reason is that the men have always had some task that was obviously important and that they took seriously. Either they have been actively engaged in combat or, more recently, training for the next phase of the war, namely the invasion of Japan. Now they

---

[7] Celia Stopnicka Rosenthal, "Deviation and Social Change in the Jewish Community of a Small Polish Town," *American Journal of Sociology* (September 1954), 60:177–181.

[8] *Ibid.*, p. 181, quoted from Merton, *Social Theory and Social Structure* (italics Merton's).

[9] Rosenthal, *op. cit.*, p. 180.

introduction to anomie theory

know this invasion is not going to come off, and that they will eventually be returning home. But we know this is going to take a long time. There are millions of men to be returned to the States, thousands of tons of equipment to be disposed of or shipped back in an orderly manner, and many other transitional functions to be performed. This will take a long time, and in the meantime this outfit may find itself sitting on its haunches for months with no assigned mission. The men will chafe and grow restive; they will not be interested in continuing to practice mortar firing and digging foxholes; discipline will break down and we shall have men going AWOL. We must anticipate and forestall this development. We will immediately turn this battalion into a school, and I am putting you in charge. Mornings will be given over entirely to classes, afternoons to organized recreational activities and physical training. You will offer courses in any subjects in which the men are interested, whether they be English composition, carpentry, photography, or trigonometry. You will select your faculty from the battalion personnel and you will obtain the necessary equipment. Do you have any questions? Good day!

The battalion commander was prophetic. There was a severe crisis in morale in the Philippines, and a general breakdown in discipline, with public marches and demonstrations bordering on mutiny, and a great increase in AWOL's. To my knowledge this battalion commander was the only unit commander who took the steps that he did. His goal was clearly in the interest of the Army and in fulfillment of his obligations as a unit commander.

The achievement of the goal, however, was not that simple. The mission for which chemical mortar battalions were created was to provide mortar support in combat operations. An elaborate system of War Department directives, memoranda, and tables of organization and equipment (T/O and E) specified in great detail what each type of unit was entitled to in the way of supplies and equipment, and in what quantities and at what intervals, and prescribed elaborate clerical and bookkeeping procedures for ordering, issuing, and keeping track of supplies. It goes without saying that things cannot be otherwise, when everything is in short supply and some method must be found for allocating scarce goods among a multitude of would-be users. It was not contemplated by the architects of the military organization that a chemical mortar battalion might, under certain conditions, best serve the interests of the Army by functioning like a junior college, and practically none of the equipment needed for this hastily improvised school was authorized by any regulations.

However, the school quickly materialized, and so did the necessary equipment. I spent one day a week traveling about the island of Luzon, "requisitioning" equipment. ("Requisitioning," as practiced in the armed services, can mean (1) properly requesting, (2) confiscating, or (3) just plain stealing—sometimes referred to as "liberating.") This day was dedicated to the violation of regulations, not only by me but by scores of supply sergeants and officers in dozens of Army, Navy, and Air Force installations. Requests were not granted perfunctorily: I had to explain my bizarre requests for cameras and other photographic equipment; for books, automobile engines, stationery, and so on. But when I did this, I met with understanding and cooperation. Of course this procurement activity was largely furtive, involving a great deal of illegal falsification of records, and it was not without some risk to those involved. But the school was successful. (Some months later the War Department caught up with events and issued regulations authorizing the issuance of supplies that I had only been able to obtain illegally.)

Let us now consider this episode in the light of anomie theory. The goal in this instance was an *organizational* one (not simply the success aspirations of so many discrete individuals), although the executors of the goal were individuals

79

acting in their official capacities as agents of the organization. Nobody disputed the legitimacy of the goal; although it was not spelled out in the regulations, it could easily be justified in terms of the larger goals of the Army. However, if the normative rules were followed, the goal was clearly impossible of attainment. The "adaptation" was, in terms of Merton's paradigm, a case of innovation on the organizational level.

It might be argued that nobody regarded what was being done as "really wrong," in view of the exceptional circumstances, and that this is not, therefore, a genuine case of deviance. This raises an important and legitimate question. The same question can be raised about many other examples of "patterned evasion of normative rules." such as the wholesale granting of divorces in circumstances not authorized by the law; and the failure of law enforcement officials to enforce certain of the laws regulating sexual conduct.[10] Certainly these cases are deviant only in an equivocal sense, and yet it is not true that the normative rules in question are "dead letters," to be simply and blandly ignored. In the present instance, for example, they were *furtively* evaded, not openly flouted. If attention of "responsible officials" had been publicly called to what was going on, they would have felt constrained to "do something about it," and in fact it was, as we have said, not without risk.

We have encountered here one of the classical dilemmas of all bureaucratic organizations: What to do when the normative rules of the organization, designed to facilitate the realization of its goals, instead get in their way. It is not satisfactory to have a general understanding that anyone may with impunity violate the rules whenever in his judgment it would, on balance, further the ends of the organization, for it is precisely one of the intended functions of the rules to restrict the exercise of personal judgment. In the Army, in fact, people were always being reprimanded, or more drastically punished, for substituting their own judgment and common sense for the prescribed "G. I. way." On the other hand, not to turn the blind eye occasionally to violations of the rules can be damaging or even suicidal to the organization. The patterned evasion that we sometimes get is not, then, a simple and automatic reflex to rigid and frustrating rules. It is complex, subtle, fitful, sometimes tortuous, and usually incomplete.

Illustration:
A Governmental Bureaucracy

Blau analyzed the operations of a department in the public employment agency of an Eastern state.[11] The agency's "major responsibility is to serve workers seeking employment and employers seeking workers." [12] The tasks of interviewers included interviewing clients, helping them to fill out application forms, counseling with them, and referring them to jobs—taking into account the requirements of the job and the interests and qualifications of the client. From the standpoint of the organization, these specific tasks were instrumental to the "major responsibility." However, as in any organization, and especially as in large, complex, and busy bureaucracies, there was the problem of keeping track of the performance of interviewers, for purposes of control and of evaluation of individual and group performance; a complex organization cannot function effectively without feedback (to supervisors) of such statistically con-

10 For an excellent discussion see Robin M. Williams, *American Society: A Sociological Interpretation*, 2nd ed. (New York: Knopf, 1960), pp. 372–391.
11 Peter M. Blau, *The Dynamics of Bureaucracy* (Chicago: The University of Chicago Press, 1955).
12 *Ibid.*, p. 19.

introduction to anomie theory

solidated information. To this end, various systems of statistical records were used at various times. However, every system of record-keeping is selective; it highlights certain aspects of performance and overlooks others, and a "good rating" is likely to mask behavior inconsistent with the goals of the organization and the behavior expected of the employees. Blau provides numerous examples, some of them flat violations of the rules of the organization, and comments:

> An instrument intended to further the achievement of organizational objectives, statistical records constrained interviewers to think of maximizing the indices as their major goal, sometimes at the expense of these very objectives. They avoided operations which would take up time without helping them to improve their record, such as interviewing clients for whom application forms had to be made out, and wasted their own and the public's time on activities intended only to raise the figures on their record. Their concentration upon this goal, since it was important for their ratings, made them unresponsive to requests from clients that would interfere with its attainment.[13]

Blau does not formulate his analysis specifically in terms of Merton's model. In point of fact, it invites attention to complications that a straightforward application of Merton's model does not take account of; but this makes it all the more instructive for our purposes. Let us break this analysis down into its components—some of them explicit, some of them only implied.

(1) The rules of the system—its "culture structure"—specify, for each position, without regard to the personalities who happen to occupy it, goals and a set of procedures for attaining them.

(2) But the *interests* of the position occupant, although they may include the goals and norms of the culture structure, will surely extend beyond them. These other interests may derive from his long-range aspirations, his involvement in systems outside the immediate organization, his interaction with other employees in the work situation, and hopes, fears, and expectations resulting from his previous socialization. They will include such things as security of tenure, good relationships with fellow workers, high wages, and prospects of promotion.

(3) Action that conforms to the normative rules and is adequate to the realization of the culture goals may or may not satisfy these other interests. Therefore, we have another source of strain or disjunction that we should distinguish from that which Merton seems to have in mind. But the actor's behavior is governed by his total interest-set, and an adaptation that resolves his *personal* problem may violate the rules of the organization.

(4) The consequences of any course of action depend partly on the *rewards and punishments* his supervisors mete out for it. This in turn depends on *which aspects of his performance are visible to them*, and *this* depends upon the mechanisms for feeding back to them information about his performance. We may call this the *incentive structure* of the organization.

(5) In the present instance, Blau does not suggest that the institutionalized means are not adequate to the attainment of the culture goals, but that, because of the incentive structure, the culture structure is not fully integrated with the interests of the position occupants. The resultant behavior does not quite fit any of Merton's modes of adaptation. It most nearly resembles his "ritualism," but it is not simply a blind devotion to means without regard to their ends. It is a selective emphasis upon those institutionalized means that best serve the actor's important interests, which interests may include but are not exhausted by the culture goals.

[13] *Ibid.*, p. 43. See also Joseph Bensman and Bernard Rosenberg, *Mass, Class, and Bureaucracy* (Englewood Cliffs, N.J.: Prentice-Hall, 1963), Chap. 10, especially pp. 307–309.

81

Other examples come readily to mind. In the public schools, for example, the culture structure may emphasize academic instruction, character development, individualized attention to the needs of each child, and so on. But the aspect of the teacher's performance that may be most visible to the principal may be his effectiveness in maintaining order and discipline in the classroom. This may be useful or even necessary for the achievement of the aforementioned goals, but in teachers' meetings the principal may explicitly and very likely sincerely emphasize that it is merely a means and not to be exalted into an end in itself. However, the incentive structure may be such that the teacher's interests are best served by gross neglect of what all agree are the "real goals" of his position, and by overconformity to a "mere means."

Illustration:
The Soviet Firm [14]

In the planned economy of the Soviet Union, production targets for each firm are not determined by the market, as we understand the term, but by central planning agencies. These targets specify in considerable detail the kinds of goods to be produced, and their quantities (quality is more difficult to specify, but it is understood that the goods will be of good quality). The allocation of resources and raw materials is likewise determined, as it is in military organizations, not by the free play of the market but by decisions of a central planning agency. As in military organizations, requisitions must be justified by some kind of documentary authorization, and detailed procedures are prescribed. Underfulfillment of the plan may be severely punished; overfulfillment may be rewarded by substantial bonuses to both managers and workers. In fact, bonuses play much the same function in the Soviet system that profits do in owner-operated enterprises in the American system.

However, it is difficult and sometimes impossible to fulfill precisely quantified production targets, and at the same time turn out goods of acceptable quality, and still conform to specified operational procedures, especially those relating to the procurement of capital resources and raw materials. According to one student of the subject:

> ... the bonus system is an effective device for eliciting a high level of managerial effort, but in the context of excessively high production targets, it induces management to make certain types of decisions that are contrary to the intent of the state. The production of unplanned products, the concealment of production capacity, the falsification of reports and the deterioration of quality are the unintended consequences of the system of managerial incentives.[15]
>
> ... the incentives that motivate managers to strive for the fulfillment of their production targets are the same incentives that motivate them to evade the regulations of the planning system. Because of the tightness of the supply system ... managers are compelled to defend their enterprise's position by overordering supplies, by hoarding materials and equipment, and by employing expediters

[14] The sources upon which this section is based deal with the Soviet system prior to 1960. Since then, important changes have occurred in the economies of the Soviet Union and other Eastern European communist countries, and what we have to say here may no longer be so applicable. See Joseph S. Berliner, "The Informal Organization of the Soviet Firm," *The Quarterly Journal of Economics* (August 1952), 66:342–365; Joseph S. Berliner, "The Situation of Plant Managers," in Alex Inkeles and Kent Geiger (eds.), *Soviet Society: A Book of Readings* (Boston: Houghton Mifflin, 1961), pp. 361–381; and David Granick, *The Red Executive* (Garden City, New York: Doubleday, 1961).

[15] Berliner, "The Situation of Plant Managers," p. 369.

whose function it is to keep the enterprise supplied with materials at all costs, legal or otherwise.[16]

The purpose of this example is not to point up the imperfections of the Soviet system in contrast to the virtues of the American system. Berliner, the author we have just quoted, goes on to:

> . . . caution the reader once more against inferring from this that the Soviet managers do not do a *good* job. They do. There is no doubt that their system works well. If I have chosen to concentrate on the "pathology" of Soviet management, the purpose was not to create the impression of ineffectiveness, but to illuminate the gap that every economy shows between the actual and the ideal.[17]

Many of the irregular or illegal practices in the Soviet system have very precise counterparts in the American system, reflecting certain similarities in the social organization, the incentive structures, and the environments of the industrial organization in both countries. In addition, each country seems to generate its own characteristic forms of deviance, reflecting differences in the structure of the respective economies. The Soviet system is especially productive of deviance in the area of procurement. The American system, by contrast, is admirably contrived to encourage deviance on an enormous scale in the area of merchandising.

In this chapter we have not limited ourselves to studies selfconsciously formulated in terms of the anomie tradition. We are not so much interested in terminologies as in the underlying explanatory model. In our final chapter we will return to more recent developments in anomie theory.

[16] *Ibid.*, p. 371.
[17] *Ibid.*, p. 374.

group support:
what are
the others doing?

eight

Anomie theory asks: "What do people want? What are the rules regulating their choice of means? What means are, in fact, legitimately available to them? How does deviance reduce the strain resulting from wanting something that is not legitimately obtainable?" We turn now to a number of other approaches in the sociological tradition, all of which ask: "How do deviance and conformity depend on what *other* people think, say, feel, and do?" Briefly summarized, these approaches deal with the ways in which action in general, and deviant action in particular, is determined by the ways in which people are cognitively, morally, relationally, and materially dependent upon other people.

Varieties of Dependence
Influencing Deviance and Control

Cognitive and Moral Dependence

This refers to the idea that people's knowledge, beliefs, and values—their notions about what is, what is possible, and what is right— depend upon other people's knowledge, beliefs, and values. It means that if we want to understand what goes on in a person's mind, our starting point should be what goes on in the minds of the people around him. This is the essence of what we mean by culture; the infant in the household and the novitiate in a social group, if they are to survive as social beings, must do business with others, and to do this they must "take the role of the other," see things through other people's eyes, adopt their perspectives and make them their own. Culture is not, however, a homogeneous stock of ideas shared uniformly throughout society. Within a society there are many variants of the common culture, and even cultures in some measure opposed to the larger culture. These are *subcultures,* and the ideas of any particular individual are derived from the subcultures to which he is most exposed and with which he most strongly identifies.

In a slightly different way, this cognitive and moral dependence is also the theme of "reference-group theory." [1] Reference-group theory emphasizes the uncertainty and instability of men's beliefs when they cannot check these against the beliefs of others; they hold most firmly those beliefs that they share with others. But not just *any* others. For each of us, what *certain* groups or perhaps individuals believe carries a special authority. These are our reference groups or persons. Each of us has a somewhat different set of reference objects who play an especially decisive role in shaping our thinking.

If we think of deviant behavior as behavior guided by beliefs and values at variance with those of the dominant groups in society, then the explanation of deviance is a special case of the explanation of the transmission of culture or the influence of reference groups. Individuals commit deviant acts because they have learned the supporting beliefs and values, from subcultures in which they have participated, in the same way people learn conventional beliefs and values from *their* subcultures, and they are sustained in this behavior by the agreement and approval of their reference groups. Social organization determines the distribution of deviant behavior and conformity by structuring the networks of social interaction in which reference groups are acquired and cultural learning occurs.

Relational Dependence

By this we mean the need to establish certain kinds of social relationships with others. Such are the needs to be liked, loved, admired, respected, wanted, nurtured, protected, dominated, deferred to. We need not assume that all men have the same relational needs, certainly not in the same degree. But it is an inescapable consequence of growing up in a social setting that all men become sensitized to *some* kinds of attitudes on the part of others. Once this sensitivity has been established, the granting or withholding of certain kinds of social relationships becomes the most powerful reward or punishment that man can administer; to act in such a way as to elicit the kinds of relationships one values becomes one of the most powerful motives of human conduct.

By and large, relational rewards are earned by behaving in a way that is valued by other people, by satisfying *their* needs or conforming to *their* expectations. To some degree, men manipulate these rewards more or less consciously to control the behavior of others. For the most part, however, the distribution of relational rewards is not calculated and deliberate. There is nothing more obvious to us, when we are confident in our own beliefs, than that those who dispute them, by word or deed, are either ignorant, stupid, or vicious; we respond to them quite spontaneously with anger, ridicule, contempt, or outright rejection.

From one point of view, the quest for satisfying social relationships can be viewed as a process of exchanging conformity for relational rewards. This *process* is the same whether the group that administers the rewards is conventional or deviant, although the *content* of the exchange is different. Indeed, one of the most common explanations of juvenile delinquency, in both the professional literature and the world of everyday life, is a straightforward application of this model: A boy, seeking to satisfy the same basic needs for acceptance, companionship, and respect as other boys, is unable to obtain these from conventional groups because he cannot meet the terms on which they are granted; he turns to other groups

---

[1] See Robert K. Merton, *Social Theory and Social Structure* (Glencoe, Ill.: The Free Press, 1949), Chaps. 8 and 9.

85

whose terms—participating in their delinquent way of life—he can more easily meet.

To emphasize the distinction between the two kinds of dependence we have discussed: the first refers to our dependence on agreement with others for cognitive and moral *certainty*; the second refers to dependence upon conformity to others' expectations for emotional or relational *security*.

Material Dependence

By this we refer to the fact that most human actions are like moves in games: standing by themselves, out of context, they are but fragments of action—broken, meaningless, futile. They make sense only as part of a larger activity which is constructed by fitting together and joining, so to speak, the contributions of a number of people. Nobody can hit a home run or strike out all alone in an empty field, but only in a game context; nor can he "take" an examination simply by sitting down and proceeding to fill an examination booklet: there must be somebody to "give" it. And if meaning depends on other people making their moves, playing their parts, still more does *effect*. Whatever it is we seek to accomplish, the acts that we ourselves perform contribute only part of the effort necessary to bring it about. Whenever we set about doing something, it is on the assumption that somebody else, because he feels obligated or it is to his interest, will do whatever else is necessary. Pursuing a goal is largely a matter of doing what one must in order to insure that other people will produce the acts that we require of them.

This means that most human behavior, deviant behavior included, requires organization; that it is performed in company or that it is a link in a chain of action which others must complete; that it therefore depends on common understandings and trust; and that wickedness, no less than virtue, must find confederates and fit itself into an organized system of action in order to bear fruit. Here too the model of exchange is applicable. To get others to do what we require of them, we must do something that is useful to them.

If the participants in an organized system of action need one another's help in order to realize their own ends, then each has some measure of power over the others, although some are more powerful than others. This power is evident not only in action but also in inaction. By refraining from doing what one can do, by withholding reciprocity, one can rob the other's action of its effect. The exercise of power, whether by acting or not acting, is an instrument for compelling cooperation, whether in the interest of control or deviance. Blackmail is a crude and obvious example.

The Influences of Dependence:
Some Examples and Applications

In some of the examples we shall present, one or another of the foregoing types of dependence may be especially prominent. Where this is so, it is because the treatment itself is fragmentary. The intensive analysis of almost any kind of deviance is likely to reveal that it is on the one hand sustained, on the other hand threatened, by all these types of dependence.

Homosexuality and Drug Addiction

Our emphasis here is not on the origins of the respective types of deviance, on "how people get that way." It is rather on the ways in which one's relationships with others makes possible the deviant way of life. In both we have what is essentially a "community of deviants," a number of people who have

group support: what are the others doing?

in common a propensity to some activity that is stigmatized and penalized by the larger society. In both are found the following: (1) a measure of withdrawal from active and intimate association with the world of "respectable" and "conventional" people, and heightened involvement in a world of fellow pariahs; (2) reduced dependence upon the nondeviant world for reference-group support, relational security, and material satisfactions; (3) a culture that provides a normative basis for the behavior stigmatized by the nondeviant world; (4) a system of social relations that provides some of the relational security denied to these deviants by the nondeviant world; (5) cooperation and exchange in the pursuit of deviant behavior and material satisfactions; and (6) techniques for neutralizing threats to the deviant way of life from the outside world. They also differ according to the specific requirements of the type of deviance and the attitudes of the conventional environment, but both must provide some solutions, however imperfect, to the same set of problems.

Homosexuality, like bridge, tennis, and intercourse duly licensed by the church and city hall, requires some sort of interaction with like-minded people. Homosexuals must learn to find and recognize other homosexuals, to sound out one another, and to come to understandings. They develop a language of word and gesture unintelligible to the "straight" world. They have places to meet and places to congregate, where they may relax and be their homosexual selves, sheltered from the curious or censorious eyes of the "straight" people. They develop understandings regulating homosexual relationships, for homosexuality, like the more legitimate forms of sexual activity, is rife with the potentialities of disruptive competition and conflict. But not all homosexuals are equally immersed in this homosexual community; much depends on the degree to which they still have emotional and material stakes in their relationships with the conventional world. The greater these stakes, the more peripheral, sporadic, and furtive their participation in the homosexual community and its culture, because open and obvious involvement in the homosexual community may mean total degradation and denial of social and occupational opportunity in the heterosexual community. Some participate more fully, openly, and continuously in the homosexual community: these have liquidated their emotional and material investments, so to speak, in the heterosexual community; they are less dependent upon it, and have re-invested in the homosexual community.[2]

Even if homosexuality were regarded as a perfectly legitimate form of sexual behavior, homosexuals would no doubt form somewhat distinctive social groupings on the basis of their common interests, as do such diverse types as jazz buffs, bird-watchers, and physicians. However, inasmuch as being known as a homosexual does not result in denial of the right to participate on an equal footing in the conventional world, there is no need for a homosexual community radically segregated from the conventional world and providing for a wide range of satisfactions withheld by the conventional world.

Most of what we have said about the homosexual community applies to the world of narcotics addicts and need not be repeated, but there are differences. One can not satisfy the need for narcotics without the cooperation of others any more than he can satisfy the need for tennis or the need to publish a book. Furthermore, once he is "hooked," the narcotics addict's need for drugs is more imperious and more regular than almost any other human need. However, in a country like England, where addiction is not a crime, where it is defined as a medical rather than a police problem, and where a maintenance dosage can be

2 See Maurice Leznoff and William A. Westley, "The Homosexual Community," *Social Problems* (April 1956), 3:257–263; and Edwin M. Schur, *Crimes Without Victims* (Englewood Cliffs, N.J.: Prentice-Hall, 1965), pp. 67–119.

group support: what are the others doing?

purchased at nominal cost on the prescription of a physician, the situation of the addict resembles more closely that of the diabetic than it does that of the addict in this country. Addiction as such does not result in exclusion from the world of "decent people," nor does the acquisition of the drug require an elaborate network of extra-legal and illegal activities. In the United States, by contrast, the addict's craving for drugs cannot, except in rare instances, be legally satisfied; illegal ways of obtaining the drug are dangerous and enormously expensive; and addiction itself consigns one, in most social circles, to the status of an outcast. The community that arises, quite predictably, in response to this narcotics situation, includes not only addicts but also wholesalers and retailers of illegal drugs, as well as some law-enforcement officers who also have a valuable commodity (nonenforcement) that is in great demand and that can command a large price. This is not a tight-knit and solidary community. It is under too constant harassment and the consequences of being arrested are too drastic to permit large and stable groupings. However, the addict's need for the drug is so urgent that he cannot manage without addict friends and without learning his way about, if only as a customer, in the underworld of the narcotics trade. Because preoccupation with ways and means of obtaining the drug is so disruptive of ordinary lawful ways of making a living, and because the drug is so expensive, the addict is usually compelled to steal or to cultivate some other "hustle" in order to obtain the wherewithal to purchase it, and this pushes him into a still deeper dependence upon the loose-knit community of mutually suspicious yet mutually indispensable addicts. But this community is more than just a set of arrangements to facilitate obtaining drugs; it is also, to a degree, a moral community that jointly supports a culture that gives meaning, a certain amount of status, and some legitimacy to the way of life that revolves around the drug.[3]

"Krugovaya Poruka"

This Russian expression (sometimes rendered "krugovaia poruka") may be loosely translated as "group support." In the Soviet factory it refers to mutual aid among members of a group whose members feel some sense of solidarity, mutual responsibility, and mutual dependence, especially if this aid is outside of or in outright violation of the formal rules of the organization. It has an affinity with the word "blat," which signifies influence, connections, an "in" with somebody. In the last chapter we discussed some of the pressures toward deviance in the Soviet factory, and some forms this deviance took. But deviance does not immediately emerge because it is somehow useful or convenient to somebody. We have emphasized that successful deviance usually requires the active assistance or the acquiescence of others, both in its performance and in the evasion of detection and punishment. But others must be motivated to render this assistance. This is likely to occur: when a number of people depend upon one another in important ways to begin with, such as the proper completion of their respective tasks in the division of labor; when, at any given time, several of them have burdens that could be lightened or problems that could be solved by violating the rules; and when it is probable that, sooner or later, almost anybody *might* find himself with such burdens or problems. *Krugovaya poruka* implies, of course, an expectation of reciprocity, not in the sense of strict accounting and precise equivalence of *quid pro quo*, but in the sense of "let us all live together in peace

[3] See Schur, *op. cit.*, pp. 120–168, and *Narcotic Addiction in Britain and America: The Impact of Public Policy* (Bloomington: Indiana University Press, 1962); Lindesmith, *The Addict and the Law*; and *Drug Addiction: Crime or Disease?* Interim and Final Reports of the Joint Committee of the American Bar Association and the American Medical Association on Narcotic Drugs (Bloomington: Indiana University Press, 1961).

group support: what are the others doing?

and help one another as the occasion arises." It implies also the threat of withdrawal of reciprocity: "If you want to get along, you had better play along. You need us as badly as we need you." A senior engineer reported:

Sometimes the molds were badly made, and this resulted in a certain part being too heavy. Therefore, the final product will weigh 14 tons instead of 10 tons. I have to explain this error, but I cannot say that it was due to bad work. I must say that tests show that this added strength is necessary. The director will call in the chief design engineer to confirm this statement. He will have to confirm this or everybody will get into trouble, and he is too small a man to object. If he should refuse to do it, the chief engineer and the director will remember this and he will never get a premium [bonus] again. If he ever gets into any minor trouble, they will make it very hard for him. The chief design engineer often gets into trouble, because his work is difficult and experimental, and he makes many mistakes. Therefore, he must be on good relations with the director, else they will "bury him" one day for one of his inevitable mistakes. . . . This mutual relationship is called *krugovaia poruka*. It is very hard to free yourself of it. You can get out of it only if the minister transfers you to another factory.[4]

It is obvious that this is not a Russian invention. A large part of the American literature on industrial sociology, especially that part dealing with informal organization, is concerned with *krugovaya poruka*. Informal organization refers to the rules that emerge spontaneously among groups of workers who are thrown together by the circumstances of the job. These rules partly supplement, partly thwart, the official rules. These workers depend upon one another in all the ways we have described, and more, and by exploiting the power that this dependence entails, they secure conformity to the rules of the informal organization and may nullify management's efforts at control.[5]

Krugovaya poruka often comes to embrace those very individuals whose office is to prevent and expose it. This is because those individuals, by virtue of *their* job, are thrown into interaction with those they are supposed to police, and in various degrees often become dependent upon them. This may be the simple relational dependence that normally develops among any people who regularly do business with one another, or it may be a deep and many-sided dependence. In the Soviet Union, for example, the resident member of the commissariat, the government department responsible for the performance of the firm, is an agent of control, but he is likely to become personally friendly with the plant officials and dependent upon their cooperation and good will. The circle of *krugovaya poruka* tends to widen and swallow him up.[6] Zawodny comments on the tendency of *krugovaya poruka* to come to embrace a diverse set of officials, each of whom is supposed to function as a check and monitor on the others: "The secretary of the all-plant Party committee, the director of the plant, the chairman of the all-plant trade union committee, and the chief accountant seem the most effective combination for the practice of *blat* and *krugovaya poruka*, because in their hands are the instruments for the control of power."[7]

The position of foreman in American factories has frequently been analyzed

[4] Joseph S. Berliner, "The Informal Organization of the Soviet Firm," *The Quarterly Journal of Economics* (August 1952), 66:359.
[5] For an excellent analysis see George C. Homans, *The Human Group* (New York: Harcourt, Brace, 1950), Chaps. 1–6. Homans' "internal system" is roughly, although not precisely, the equivalent of "informal organization." See also Bensman and Rosenberg, *op. cit.*, pp. 303–305.
[6] *Ibid.*, pp. 359–360.
[7] Janusz K. Zawodny, *Settlement of Workers' Grievances in Soviet Factories*, Ph.D. thesis, Stanford University, 1955, p. 68.

group support: what are the others doing?

in these same terms. He has power over his crew, and they must defer to him, but they have many ways of making trouble for him, and so he must cooperate with them and overlook some of their violations of rules.

But *krugovaya poruka* is not peculiar to the factory. Even the prison guard tends to be drawn into a system of mutually advantageous exchange with those he is guarding.[8] The starting point for the analysis of this system is a phenomenon common to many organizational positions: a span of responsibility wider than the span of legitimate control. That is, the prison guard (like the policeman, the Army officer, the foreman, the district sales manager) is expected by "top management" to produce results that he sometimes cannot deliver with the means legitimately available to him. He is expected to maintain order and discipline among the inmates, and secure compliance with numerous and detailed rules. But the social distance between the inmates on the one hand, and the guards and the administration the guards represent, is so great; the conflict of interests between the inmates, concerned with maximizing their autonomy and privileges, and the guards, concerned with enforcing a repressive regimen, is so sharp; the inmates are so many and the guards are so few—that it is impossible for the guards to satisfy their superiors' demands for effective custody and control simply by ordering and forbidding and by administering the authorized rewards and punishments. Faced with this problem, the guards tend to enter into a set of implicit understandings with the inmates. They make life easier for the inmates by neglecting the enforcement of some rules in exchange for compliance with others. Furthermore, they make special concessions to some of the inmates who are influential within the inmate body, and even enhance this influence by giving them access to information, food, and other commodities that may be exchanged with other inmates. These privileged inmates use their influence to help prevent the more visible and flagrant violations of the prison rules, the sorts of violations that are most likely to get the guards into trouble. From one point of view this is the corruption of the guards; from another it is *krugovaya poruka*.

Further Implications for Control

This enlargement of the circle of *krugovaya poruka* is not the only way in which controls originating outside the system, or on a superordinate level of the system, may be weakened or nullified. Even where agents of external control are untainted by this kind of collusion, their efforts at control are not likely to be highly successful if they cannot obtain the cooperation of the group they are supposed to control. This is true whether we are speaking of police, deans of students, commanding officers of military units, or federal regulatory agencies. To be effective in discovering deviance, and in apprehending and punishing deviants, they all need complainants, informants, witnesses, and sometimes physical or material assistance. If they confront, not isolated deviants, but individuals who are members of more or less solidary groups or collectivities, and these groups are determined to withhold cooperation and to protect their deviant members, enforcement becomes difficult or impossible. It is worth summarizing the reasons why groups may be motivated to act in this way.

(1) In our earlier section on collectivity deviance (pp. 21-23), we observed that a number of people may share a common identity, so that what one of them does not only besmirches or enhances his good name, but that of those who are

---

[8] Probably the best analysis of this extremely complex system of exchange and mutual accommodation is "Social Control in the Prison," in Richard A. Cloward, *et al.*, *Theoretical Studies in Social Organization of the Prison* (New York: Social Science Research Council, March 1960), pp. 20–48.

group support: what are the others doing?

associated or identified with him. Those who are likely to be damaged by helping to establish the guilt of another are not likely to cooperate enthusiastically in bringing him to justice. Still less are they likely to take initiative in bringing the deviant behavior of their members to the attention of a wider public, even though the members of the "in-group" disapprove of that behavior. It is not considered good form for members of groups to "wash their dirty linen in public"; it is better to handle it within the group.

(2) We have mentioned the mechanism of reciprocity: if the guiltless members of the group feel that they *may*, at some time and for whatever reason (including their own potential deviant actions), need the help of their deviant colleagues, they will be reluctant to alienate them by assisting in their discovery and prosecution.

(3) It may not be only a fine and noble thing to bring to justice a total stranger; it is also relatively painless. But to do the same to somebody to whom we are tied by bonds of solidarity and friendship is to incur the hostility of somebody whose good opinion we have come to value.

It does not follow, however, that one may always count on the members of his in-group for support in violating the norms of the more inclusive system. On the contrary, the most potent incentives to conform may come from the in-group itself. The most obvious case is the situation in which behavior that conforms to the rules also serves the felt interests of the in-group. For example, the chemical mortar battalion described in the last chapter was engaged, during the last months of the war, in training for the anticipated invasion of Japan. On the basis of the experience of this battalion, this was expected to be a difficult and dangerous operation—costly in human lives, and requiring of all members of the unit a high degree of discipline and mastery of their respective tasks. The informal pressures from the work groups itself reinforced, without equivocation, the demands of the officers wherever these were seen as reasonably related to success and survival in the forthcoming operation.

In general terms, the in-group may assist in controlling and punishing deviance, rather than in protecting the deviant, when control and punishment rather than protection serve the collective interest of the group as a whole. Three conditions are especially relevant: the visibility of the deviant behavior, the public identification of the offender with the group, and the severity of the sanctions that the group, as distinguished from the individual offender, is likely to experience.

Where the deviant behavior is not likely to be visible outside the in-group, the norms of the in-group are likely to emphasize the obligations of the members to keep it invisible, rather than to repress it. On the other hand, where the behavior is highly visible outside the in-group, and efforts to conceal it or deny it are not likely to be successful, the in-group is more likely to try to repress the behavior itself. Thus, on campuses where university or fraternity regulations forbid drinking, the informal norms in many fraternities do not forbid drinking, but may, on the contrary, encourage it, so long as it is not visible to the "wrong" people. In like manner, conduct "unbecoming an officer and a gentleman" may be the order of the day in the officers' barracks or officers' club. In both cases, however, the same behavior that is tolerated or encouraged in the confined setting of the in-group may be severely sanctioned if carried on in public places.

How severely it will be sanctioned, however, depends not only on the visibility of the act but on the visibility of *the actor as a representative of the group*. If, for example, although the setting is public, the misbehaving student is not readily identifiable as a member of the fraternity, or the misbehaving officer is not recognizable as an officer because he is out of uniform, the misconduct is not readily gen-

91

eralizable to the group, and the group is less threatened by it. Where identification with the group is easy, the informal norms of the group tend to be harsh on the offender.

Finally, the consequences to the group of the individual's misconduct depend on the damage that the audience, or the authorities to whom the behavior is reported, can do to the group as a whole. We will shift now to a different example. The "individual" here is a firm engaged in some line of business; the "group" is the community of such firms, usually organized in a trade association. A very common sequence of events is as follows. Certain practices in violation of the law or of widespread sentiments of propriety (like excessive funeral charges or suppression of data about pharmaceutical drugs) are commonplace within the group, and are either suffered by or supported by the group as a whole. These practices may be well-known to certain publics (for example, the consumers), and may even be protested, but these publics are relatively impotent to inflict any real damage on either the offending individual or the group. At some point, however, the misconduct or illegal behavior comes to the official attention of a Congressional committee or one of the federal regulatory commissions. The misbehavior is widely publicized, proposals are made that the *group* be subject to detailed regulation (in some respect in which it has hitherto been autonomous) by some public body, and that this body be empowered to inflict severe sanctions. Representatives of the trade association then hasten to minimize the extent of the misconduct, to protest that "the industry" should not be judged by the behavior of "a few unrepresentative offenders," and to declare both the capacity and the will of the industry to police itself. The trade association promptly establishes a code, or adds new provisions to the existing code, condemning the behavior in question, and sets up its own agency to enforce it. If it acts swiftly enough, and with enough show of serious intent, it may head off obnoxious legislation or administrative regulations. This self-regulation may be highly effective for an extended period of time, or it may produce only a temporary abatement of the prohibited behavior. Frequently it is the latter, in which case, after some sort of interval (at least "until the heat is off"), the whole cycle may repeat itself.

group support: what are the others doing?

culture, role,
and interaction
process

nine

The three types of theories we are about to consider are not so different from one another as the fact of separate treatment might suggest. They do, however, have distinct emphases: the *cultural learning process* through which deviance is acquired; the ways in which *roles*, taken from the culture and incorporated into the *self*, determine deviance and conformity; and the *interaction process* within which culture is learned, roles acquired, the self built up, and patterns of deviant action shaped and transformed.

Cultural Transmission Theories

Underlying anomie theory is what we have called a conjunctive model of motivation. On the actor side is a set of goals and regulative norms acquired from his culture; on the situation side are conditions and means. Deviance arises from the interaction between the two. Cultural transmission theories place less stress on situational variables; to this extent they tend to a "kinds of people" model of motivation. (However, as we shall see, they treat situational variables as critical in the developmental or learning process.) Although this comparison, like most generalizations, distorts, it does serve to identify an important difference in emphasis.

Cultural transmission theories are also to be sharply distinguished from "kinds of people" theories of psychiatric origin. The latter tend to view the deviant act as the product of the "total personality" or "character structure." That is, the relevant intrapersonality variables may include such diverse ingredients as ego-strength, object-attachments, sex-role identifications, dependency needs, drives fixated at various developmental stages, and systems of unconscious meanings and

93

equivalences. Cultural transmission theories, while they do not deny variability in these respects, treat this variability as largely irrelevant to deviant behavior. They tend, rather, to view the motivation of a particular kind of deviant behavior as the product of knowledge and attitudes manifestly and immediately relevant to that kind of behavior. These include knowledge of the necessary techniques, moral attitudes toward the behavior in question, and definitions of particular situations as justifying or requiring that particular sort of behavior. In short, the variables that must be taken into account in order to understand deviance form a subsystem of the personality, more or less independent of other components of the personality. In this respect, these theories are not unlike commonsense theories of food preferences, which assume that fondness for chitterlings, hamburger, or scallops does not have much to do with needs for achievement, disappointment in love, attitudes toward larceny or, for that matter, the consumption of milk.

While cultural transmission theories de-emphasize the linkage between knowledge and attitudes regarding particular forms of deviance and other elements of the personality, they strongly emphasize their linkage to the corresponding knowledge and attitudes in the cultural mileu of the actor. In fact, these theories can be summarized in this way: Deviant behavior is determined by a subsystem of knowledge, beliefs, and attitudes that make possible, permit, or prescribe specific forms of deviant behavior in specific situations. This knowledge, these beliefs, and these attitudes must first exist in the cultural surroundings of the actor, and they are "taken over" and incorporated into the personality in much the same way as any other elements of the surrounding culture.

These theories, then, although they view deviants as different sorts of people from nondeviants, locate the differences in a limited segment of the personality; in other respects, deviants are like "anybody else." Furthermore, the process whereby they "get that way" is no different from the process whereby others come to be conforming members of society. We are all children of our cultures. In this way the cultural transmission theories minimize the mystery and distinctiveness of deviant behavior and maximize the common humanity of the deviant and the conformer. However, *how* people come to take over their culture, or to select from the various subcultural patterns, deviant and conventional, to which they are exposed, is not obvious. Therefore, the main theoretical issues from the point of view of these theories concern the process of cultural *learning*. In terms of the typology in Chapter 4, the research task is represented by Figure 1, b, p. 42.

Shaw and McKay

The most systematic and influential statements of cultural transmission theories were formulated by students of crime and delinquency who were trained in the sociological tradition of W. I. Thomas, Florian Znaniecki, George Herbert Mead, Robert E. Park, and Ernest W. Burgess (all associated with the University of Chicago)—a tradition often referred to as the "Chicago school" of American sociology. In a series of important monographs,[1] based mostly on research in the city of Chicago, Clifford Shaw and Henry McKay attempted to account for the distribution of delinquency in American cities. They noted that the high rate areas in Chicago in 1900-1906 were also the high rate areas

[1] Clifford R. Shaw, *The Jack-Roller* (Chicago: The University of Chicago Press, 1930); *The Natural History of a Delinquent Career* (Chicago: The University of Chicago Press, 1931); *Brothers in Crime* (Chicago: The University of Chicago Press, 1938); Clifford R. Shaw and others, *Delinquency Areas* (Chicago: The University of Chicago Press, 1929); Clifford R. Shaw and Henry D. McKay, *Social Factors in Juvenile Delinquency*, Volume II of National Committee on Law Observance and Law Enforcement, *Report on the Causes of Crime* (Washington: United States Government Printing Office, 1931); and *Juvenile Delinquency and Urban Areas* (Chicago: The University of Chicago Press, 1942).

culture, role, and interaction process

in 1917-1923, although the ethnic group composition of these areas had in the meantime been largely transformed; as ethnic groups moved in and out of these areas the delinquency rates of those ethnic groups correspondingly rose and fell. They also observed that most delinquent offenses occurred in small groups, usually of two or three, and they obtained detailed life-history materials illuminating the process of involvement in delinquent groups. They concluded that in the high-rate areas, crime and delinquency had become "more or less traditional aspects of the social life," and that "these traditions of delinquency are transmitted through personal and group contacts." [2] The chief agencies for the transmission of delinquency are the play groups and gangs. Although delinquency satisfies desires for excitment, companionship, security, and the like, this does not distinguish delinquency from nondelinquent activity. "While the standards and values" in the high-rate and low-rate areas "may be widely divergent, or even reversed, the human motives and desires underlying the boy's participation in the activities of his groups are perhaps identical in the two neighborhood situations." [3] The thing that does distinguish is the "standards and values,"—*i.e.*, the delinquent and the non-delinquent cultural patterns through which these desires are satisfied. These authors also attempt to account for the persistence of delinquent traditions in the high-rate areas in terms of the breakdown of social controls, but the core of their theory is the process of cultural transmission itself.

Edwin H. Sutherland
and the Theory of Differential Association

Edwin H. Sutherland's work, which, like that of Shaw and McKay, carries the stamp of the "Chicago school," represents the most systematic and ambitious attempt to formulate a general theory of criminal behavior in cultural transmission terms. His theory of differential association was first presented in his influential textbook, *Principles of Criminology*, and has been extended by his student and collaborator, Donald R. Cressey.[4]

The theory states that criminal behavior is learned; it is not inherited, contrived, nor invented by the actor. It is learned in a process of communication with other persons, principally in small, intimate groups. This learning includes the techniques of committing the crime and "the specific direction of motives, drives, rationalizations, and attitudes." The specific direction of motives and drives is learned from definitions of the legal codes as favorable or unfavorable. That is, those with whom we associate define the legal rules favorably or unfavorably, and we take over those definitions. A person becomes criminal or delinquent because of an excess of definitions favorable to violation of law over definitions unfavorable to violation of law. This is the principle of differential association.

Everybody has some contact with both kinds of definitions; what is decisive is the ratio of one to the other. Note that Sutherland does not speak of association with criminals and noncriminals, but rather with *definitions* favorable

[2] Shaw and McKay, *Social Factors in Juvenile Delinquency*, p. 387.
[3] *Ibid.*, p. 391.
[4] See Edwin H. Sutherland and Donald R. Cressey, *Principles of Criminology*, 6th ed. (Chicago: Lippincott, 1960) Chap. 4; Albert Cohen, Alfred Lindesmith, and Karl Schuessler (eds.), *The Sutherland Papers* (Bloomington: Indiana University Press, 1956), Part 1, pp. 5–43; and Donald R. Cressey, *Delinquency, Crime and Differential Association* (The Hague: Martinus Nijhoff, 1964). See also the commentaries by Daniel Glaser: "Differential Association and Criminological Prediction," *Social Problems* (Summer 1960), 7:2–6; "The Sociological Approach to Crime and Correction," *Law and Contemporary Problems* (Autumn 1958), 23:683–702; and "The Differential-Association Theory of Crime," in Arnold M. Rose (ed.), *Human Behavior and Social Processes: An Interactionist Approach* (Boston: Houghton Mifflin, 1962), pp. 425–442.

95

and unfavorable to crime. One may associate with few criminals, but these associations may contain many exposures to pro-criminal patterns. By the same token, however, even in his association with criminals, many kinds of criminal behavior may be unfavorably defined: the professional pickpocket may be as unsympathetic to rape, drug addiction, and wanton killing as is any conventional, high-minded citizen. On the other hand, procriminal attitudes towards (for example) income-tax evasion may be learned from people who are, on the whole, conforming and respectable. Differential associations are not all of equal weight; some have more impact than others. This weight varies with *frequency, duration, priority,* and *intensity.* If we could measure these modalities of association exactly, we would have a formula that would yield precise predictions in any particular case.

Sutherland's statement is as important for what it denies as it is for what it affirms. In particular, Sutherland denies that criminal behavior can be explained by "general needs and values." This is not because they do not help to determine criminal behavior, but because both criminal and non-criminal behavior are expressions of the same general needs and values. Thieves steal for money, honest laborers work for it. To explain differences, we must find differences.

On this level, the theory of differential association deals with the psychological question of how individuals learn criminal behavior. Turning to the sociological question of accounting for variations in rates, the theory implies that the larger culture is not homogeneous but contains contradictory definitions of the same behavior, one of which is backed by the people who make the laws. Rates and prevalence of each kind of criminal behavior depend on the way in which social organization fosters or inhibits association with criminal and anti-criminal patterns. For example, the mobility, diversity, and anonymity of urban society create more opportunities for procriminal associations than do the more controlled interaction patterns of rural society.

Sutherland's contribution is almost as important for its methodological as its substantive significance. Probably the reader's first reaction to Sutherland's theory is that it is greatly oversimplified. Surely there are a great many factors that are somehow involved in the production of criminal behavior that this theory ignores. But Sutherland did not take the position that his theory took directly into account everything that has "something to do" with criminal behavior. He was concerned with developing a *general theory*—that is, a set of propositions that identify the essential variables that are *always* involved in the learning of crime; propositions that apply without exception to the entire class of criminal behavior. There may be innumerable other circumstances that are somehow relevant to this particular instance of criminal behavior or that, but *they become relevant through the effects that they have on the variables of the theory.*

Take an analogy from medicine. An essential element of a theory to account for a certain disease includes the presence of a certain kind of germ. No germ, no disease. Now the condition of the sewer system, or the practice of drinking out of the same glass, or local climatic conditions may have something to do with the occurrence of the disease, but only because they favor the propagation or transmission of the germ. We do not expect one theory to comprehend all these things. However, we do expect the theory to make sense out of the various correlations that may be observed between the conditions like these and the occurrence of the disease, and the germ theory does this.

In strictly analogous fashion, Sutherland argues that many factors may affect crime *through their effect on associations.* The theory of differential association, however, is concerned with explaining crime, not explaining associations.

96

As a matter of fact, Sutherland was never fully satisfied with this theory, [5] though he did defend it because he felt it accounted for more of the known facts within the framework of a single, parsimonious, consistent set of propositions than any other theory. His characteristic response to criticism was to see if the theory could be modified to take the criticism into account, rather than to tack on to the theory, like so many awkward appendages, a long list of "multiple factors." We have stressed this methodological aspect of Sutherland's work because it emphasizes the distinction between the kind of systematic knowledge that is the goal of science, and a hodgepodge of loosely related ideas, curious facts, and statistical correlations.

Lack of space precludes a review of the criticisms of the theory and of research designed to test it.[6] Some of these criticisms will be noted, however, in the following section on role theory and the self.

The Self, Role Theory, and Deviant Behavior

Also characteristic of the Chicago school is a central concern with role theory and theory of the self. More than any other single person, George Herbert Mead [7] laid the foundations of these closely related lines of theory, although it has remained for others to develop their implications for deviant behavior. These theories can no longer be regarded as the property of any school; even today, however, new developments and extensions of the theory, especially as they apply to deviant behavior, are being produced chiefly by sociologists who were trained at the University of Chicago or by their students—an impressive testimony to the potency of differential association in the world of scholarship. We shall first present a brief review of some aspects of role theory and the self most relevant to our concerns, and then discuss their implications for deviant behavior.

If people are to transact business with one another—indeed if they are to deal with any aspect of the world around them—they must first identify, define, and classify; they must indicate to themselves what sort of object it is they are dealing with. Having identified it—an "antique," a "Picasso," a "mongrel," a "poker game"—some set of attitudes and expectations is called out, and it is these which largely determine what we shall do about or with the object. The categories to which we assign these objects are not present in the mind at birth, nor do they grow upon us like whiskers on the face. These categories designate the kinds of objects that things can be in *our* culture; other cultures provide different classifications. These objects include people. The socially recognized categories of people—the kinds of people that people can be in a given society— are social roles (or, when formalized, are statuses or status-positions). When we learn the role system of our society, we learn a terminology for thinking and talking about them, criteria that define them (*i.e.*, what one must be to be that sort of person), signs whereby they may be recognized, images of what these people

[5] See Sutherland's own critique of the theory in Cohen, Lindesmith, and Schuessler (eds.), *op. cit.*, pp. 30–41.
[6] See the references in the footnote to the first paragraph in this section, especially the cited works of Cressey and Glaser. See also James F. Short, Jr., "Differential Association with Delinquent Friends and Delinquent Behavior," *Pacific Sociological Review* (Spring 1958), 1:20–25; and Albert J. Reiss, Jr., and A. Lewis Rhodes, "An Empirical Test of Differential Association Theory," *The Journal of Research in Crime and Delinquency* (January 1964), 1:5–18.
[7] George Herbert Mead, *Mind, Self and Society* (Chicago: The University of Chicago Press, 1934).

97

are like, expectations about how they *should* behave, and standards for evaluating them.

The self is also a social object. It is the actor as seen, labeled, classified, and judged by the actor himself. How he feels about himself, how he conducts himself, what he tries to do with or about himself, whether he tries to change himself, depend in the first instance on what sort of object he thinks he is or wants to be. Again, the kinds of selves that are possible depend on the culture. President and bartender, citizen and alien, old man and teenager, hip and square, are part of the culturally provided repertoire of roles in American society. These roles are partly ascribed to us whether we like it or not; others are optional and open to achievement. The self is built up in the process of interacting with others. In doing business with them, we discover what we are—*i.e.*, the categories to which we have been assigned—and to some extent we determine what we shall be. We may lay claims to being a certain sort of person, but this claim must make sense in terms of the culture of those we are dealing with, and we must make these claims stick. To lay a claim is to say, in effect: "I am such-and-such a sort of person; I invite you to deal with me on this basis; you may expect certain things of me." To make the claim stick, we must validate it by meeting the cultural criteria of the role. We know we have done this when others, by their responses, indicate acceptance of us as valid specimens of the role. In so doing, we also confirm our conception of ourselves. We cannot really tell whether we are "leaders," "glamor girls," "pool sharks," or "brains" without venturing into the icy waters of social interaction, trying our hand at the role, and seeing how others respond.

Everybody is continually engaged in a lifelong process of building, maintaining, or refashioning a self. Working within the role repertoire provided by his culture, he plays at being this sort of person or that, observes his success or failure as he reads it in the responses of others, discovers whether it is hard or easy for him to carry it off, and whether it is really worth it. Whether it is worth it depends on the prestige and the other rewards, relational and material, that go with being that kind of person in the world in which he moves.

All self-building activities—experimenting with new selves, maintaining or repairing an established self, or shuffling off an old, perhaps outmoded, self—consist largely in behaving in ways that help to confirm our claims about our selves, and avoiding behavior that tends to undermine those claims. But the kinds of behavior that may confirm or weaken those claims are not a separate and distinct category of actions. Almost *anything* we do, even if it is not intended primarily as a "presentation of the self," [8] and even if the actor himself is the only witness, can be interpreted as evidence regarding the self. Therefore, whatever other ends we may have in view, almost anything we do and the manner in which we do it is chosen partly with a view to its consequences for the self.

Not all the roles with which we are identified are actively sought and cultivated. Some, like the roles of alcoholic and ex-convict, we may actively resist and deny. Some, like the role of mental patient, we may accept with passive resignation. Some, like the role of prostitute, we may adopt for practical reasons, looking forward to the time when we may exchange it for some other, less disreputable but equally remunerative occupation. Typically, however, when we cannot escape public identification with such roles and are invested with such "deviant characters," we still engage in various maneuvers to avoid subjective identification

[8] The expression is Erving Goffman's, from his book, *The Presentation of Self in Everyday Life* (Edinburgh: University of Edinburgh Social Science Research Centre Monograph, No. 2, 1956). Goffman is the most original and productive continuator of George Herbert Mead's work on role theory and the self.

culture, role, and interaction process

with the role as expressive of our "real selves"; to emphasize the secondary, temporary, and subordinate nature of the role, as compared to other, more acceptable components of the self; and to limit the visibility of the role to circles in which publicity is inescapable or the consequences less damaging.[9]

Some Implications for Deviant Behavior

Motivation. Behavior may contribute to the credibility of our role claims in various ways. On the one hand, it may demonstrate that one has the credentials of the role or that one is a first-class specimen of the role; this depends, of course, on the criteria of the role and the standards by which adequacy in the role is currently judged. Thus, to validate one's claims to being a philanthropist, one must sooner or later "put up or shut up." On the other hand, various activities that do not directly signify the possession of a role may help to make possible other activities that do. Thus, making money is not being a philanthropist, but it does provide the means for being one. Indeed, we take on some roles not because they are directly important to the self but because they facilitate the performance of other roles. Grosser [10] has distinguished behavior that contributes to role validation in two ways: as "role-expressive" and "role-supportive." He has observed that, although both boys and girls steal, boys' stealing tends to be more versatile; they steal all sorts of things from all sorts of place, and frequently steal things of no earthly use to them. Girls tend to steal things they can use—clothing, cosmetics, jewelry, and the like, mostly from stores. Grosser suggested that *stealing as such,* like "badness" in general, is expressive of, or at least compatible with, the male role in our society. One does not have to steal (or tear up property, or "raise hell") to prove he is a boy, but it is one way of demonstrating that he is "all boy," especially if it involves a certain amount of courage, daring, and defiance of authority. Girls, on the other hand, do not strengthen their claims to femininity by stealing as such. Being pretty, charming, dainty, and well-groomed, however, *is* expressive of the feminine role. Therefore, when girls steal, they tend to steal only those accoutrements and supplies that help them to be pretty, charming, and so forth. Their stealing is role-supportive. If, however, a boy should steal in order to be able to squire girls around or have money to be able to maintain a reputation for generosity, then *his* stealing would be role supportive.

A great deal of deviance that seems "irrational" and "senseless" makes some sense when we see it as an effort to proclaim or test a certain kind of self. A great deal of illicit (as well as socially acceptable) sexual activity is motivated less by glandular secretions than by role anxiety. The use of marihuana and heroin, especially the early experimental stages; driving at dangerous speeds and "playing chicken" on the highway; illegal consumption of alcoholic beverages; participation in illegal forms of social protest and civil disobedience; taking part in "rumbles"—all these are likely to be role-expressive behavior. In order to recognize this motivation, however, one must know the roles that are at stake, and what kinds of behavior carry what kinds of "role-messages" in the actor's social world.

In an earlier chapter we cited Reiss' observations that in the lower-class street corner world, engaging in fellatio did not necessarily signify, as it does in the middle class, that one is "homosexual" (see p. 32). Provided certain conditions were met, one could engage in fellatio from time to time to make a little extra money without endangering his claim to masculinity. One needs, and conceivably could compile, a "role dictionary," setting forth the role messages

[9] See Erving Goffman, *Stigma* (Englewood Cliffs, New Jersey: Prentice-Hall, 1963).
[10] George Grosser, *Juvenile Delinquency and Contemporary American Sex Roles*, Ph.D. dissertation, Harvard University, 1952.

99

that are conveyed by a given kind of behavior, deviant or otherwise, in a given social world. We would probably find that some messages that can be expressed by lawful and respectable behavior in one social level or ethnic group can, in certain circumstances, be better expressed in other social groups by illegal, "sinful," or "perverted" behavior.

One sub-type of role-supportive behavior we may call "role-protective." Cressey's analysis of embezzlement provides an example.[11] Embezzlers—that is, people who violate positions of financial trust for gain—are typically citizens of good repute. They have to be, or they would not be in these positions. In the series of cases studied by Cressey, one of the elements that was invariably present was an "unshareable problem." These were problems which, if known to others, would damage or destroy their claims to respectability. Such are sexual indiscretions for which they are being blackmailed, and financial debts growing out of gambling. Other problems that create financial hardship can be solved in legitimate ways; for example, one borrows from friends, relatives, or the bank to pay for an urgent operation for his wife or child. To do this he must make his problem more or less public, but this in no way threatens his claims to the "solid citizen" role. Faced, however, with an unshareable problem, one must find a secret way in which to obtain quite a lot of money. If the opportunity is available, he is likely to turn to role-supportive embezzlement. Even then, he cannot proceed with the act until he has hit upon some way of describing the act *to himself* in a way that is compatible with *his* self-conception. For example, he may persuade himself that he is "only borrowing" the money and not "stealing" it. One who steals is a thief, and he is unwilling to define himself as a thief. More generally, whenever one is known privily to another to have a blot on his escutcheon, he is susceptible to pressures from the other to engage with him in deviant enterprises, under threat of making public the blot and destroying the credibility of the self that he presents. Therefore, small aberrations may sometimes represent large commitments.[12] Having taken a first step towards deviance, one may not be free to retrace his steps and return to his starting point. Criminal abortion to destroy the evidence of illicit sexual activity is another example of such role-protective deviance.

Deviance, conformity, and personal roles. The selves that we present are fashioned from the role repertoire of our culture, but these selves are not standardized packages. Each self is a somewhat unique organization of roles and fragments of roles, emphasizing some claims and playing down others. These variants, adaptations, and integrations of roles we call "personal roles." We may see them evolve in the process of interaction within small groups whose members at first occupy relatively undifferentiated roles. It might be a young people's gang, a group of colleagues in an academic department, the residents of a university housing unit or fraternity. In the course of working and living together, each person tries to find out for himself a special niche, to define himself to himself and others as somebody who is especially good or dependable in some respect that matters to the other members of the group. He seeks to establish his reputation in the group as "somebody who will give you the shirt off his back," "somebody who always comes up with good ideas," "somebody who always keeps his head when others are losing theirs," "somebody who will always tell you what he honestly thinks," "somebody who will never say anything to hurt anybody," "somebody who can take a lot of ribbing," and so on.

These are roles hammered out in the give-and-take of group interaction,

[11] Donald R. Cressey, *Other People's Money: A Study of the Social Psychology of Embezzlement* (Glencoe, Ill.: The Free Press, 1953).
[12] Howard S. Becker, "Notes on the Concept of Commitment," *American Journal of Sociology* (July 1960), 66:32–40.

100

culture, role, and interaction process

and partly tailored to the strengths and resources of each member. Like other roles, we move into them gingerly, cautiously, feeling our way along because, in advancing these claims or in permitting ourselves to be so defined, we are communicating to others that we are willing to let our reputations stand or fall on certain kinds of performances. In effect, we set ourselves up as specialists of one sort or another—specialists in some art or skill, or specialists in this or that virtue. Having once committed ourselves to such a specialty, however, we feel bound, as others do not, to certain standards of excellence salient to that specialty. Some of these roles may be more highly valued by the group than others, but each is appreciated and each is rewarded. On the other hand, if we can get others to accept our claims, we can anger, offend, and disappoint them, by failing to live up to those claims, in ways that others cannot. One may pilfer supplies from the office or do less than his share of work and excite no special comment; he has advanced no claims to virtue in these respects and has staked his reputation on other sorts of performances. Others cannot do these things without inviting censure and without jeopardizing a self that has taken time and effort to establish. To reap the rewards of the roles we have succeeded in claiming, we are willing to impose upon ourselves considerable sacrifice and self-discipline. These roles are, therefore, among the most potent mechanisms of social control, although they may be completely unnoticed by what we have called the "manifest control structure" (see p. 39).

It may be appropriate here to refer again to Durkheim's statement that we find "charm in the accomplishment of a moral act," that "it has always been necessary that it appear in some respect as good" (see p. 3). Perhaps the charm of which he spoke is the feeling of exaltation and exhilaration at confirming some valued part of our identity, at discovering that we really are what we claim or hope to be. Perhaps, in this respect, it is not very different from the feeling the tennis player derives from a brilliant performance, or the fisherman from a spectacular catch.

Relations to other theories. The important variables of the theory of differential association are the frequency, duration, priority, and intensity of associations with favorable and unfavorable definitions of criminal *acts*. What we learn are attitudes, rationalizations, etc., regarding this criminal act and that. Role theory shifts the emphasis from acts to *roles*. It assumes, like differential association theory, that we do not learn anything without first being exposed to it. It also assumes, however, that whether we take notice of it, remember, and make it our own depends on whether it *matters* to us. And whatever contributes to the selves we are building, the roles we are trying to play or to which we aspire, matters. In differential association theory, the modality of "intensity" has never been satisfactorily defined; the problem of differential *susceptibility* to the same associations has never been disposed of. We are suggesting that intensity and susceptibility may depend on the role orientation of the actor. We are susceptible to those associations and learning opportunities that we sense are relevant to success in the roles we would like to assume; their impacts are more intense. Once we are "hooked" on a role, we are ready to adopt, on very slight association, whole bundles of behavior that are expressive or supportive of that role. Once we are converted to another role, we may shake off whole bundles of behavior because they are no longer consistent with the claims of the new self. From the standpoint of role theory, the central issue in the problem of learning deviant behavior becomes the process of acquiring and becoming committed to roles.[13]

[13] For the most systematic statement of a theory of criminal behavior in terms of role involvement and role committment, see Richard R. Korn and Lloyd W. McCorkle, *Criminology and Penology* (New York: Holt, 1959), pp. 327–353.

According to anomie theory, deviant behavior is a way of coping with a problem of ends and means; of reducing the tension between cultural goals and an insufficiency of institutionalized means. Role-self theory (they are so closely related as to justify a single hyphenated term) suggest another way of looking at deviance that is difficult to capture in the language of ends and means. It assumes an actor who is trying to *tell* somebody something or to *prove* something. More fitting than the language of ends and means is the language of *message* and the *symbols* that convey it, or of *claims* and *evidence*. As I have suggested elsewhere,[14] the art of seduction may be cultivated not because it is an alternative means to the goal of sexual satisfaction, but because the successful practice of the art validates a claim to being a certain sort of person. The role-expressive stealing described by Grosser is not only a means to the goal of the acquisition of objects. The novice smoking his first marihuana cigarette before a critical audience of peers is not necessarily seeking a new and more effective means to an elusive "kick." The teenager tearing down the highway at 90 miles an hour is not necessarily going anywhere.

Hardly anyone would argue that the anomie model is *not* a fruitful approach to a great deal of deviant behavior. But even where it is manifestly applicable, role theory may have something useful to contribute. For example, culture goals and normative rules are intimately connected to roles and the self. Businessmen are *supposed* to try to make money, professors to write books, and ballplayers to win games, and they are *supposed* to pursue these goals according to certain rules. In other words, the goals we seek and the means we employ themselves express and validate the roles we claim. Where there is a disjunction between goals and means, businessmen may defraud their customers, professors plagiarize, ballplayers cheat. They covertly deviate from part of the role demands in order to fulfill another part. However, there is another way sometimes open to them: *they may reduce the disjunction by abandoning the role for another role.* They can quit the game, so to speak, and find some other game at which they can win without violating the rules. This is not always possible, but it is possible often enough that it must rank among the most frequent devices for avoiding or escaping the kinds of strain that Merton is talking about. However, it is a device that does not seem to fit anywhere in Merton's typology of adaptations. It need not be deviant at all, but neither is it the kind of conformity (acceptance of goals and acceptance of means) that Merton seems to have in mind.

We are not suggesting that role-self theory displaces cultural transmission and anomie theory. Each seems to illuminate certain aspects of deviant behavior. The task for theory is to seek to integrate the contributions of each into a single, more powerful theory, without sacrificing the logical unity and discipline that are so characteristic of the work of Sutherland and Merton. We have hinted at some of the directions this work might take, and will take up this theme again in the last chapter.

Interaction Process
and Deviant Behavior

"Interaction process," as the expression was used in Chapter 4, does not refer to a type of theory in the sense in which anomie, cultural-transmission, and role-self theory do. It refers to a way of looking at action that is compatible with any of these theories, although in fact it has been most

[14] Albert K. Cohen, "The Sociology of the Deviant Act: Anomie Theory and Beyond," *American Sociological Review* (February 1965), 30:13.

culture, role, and interaction process

explicit and most highly developed in role-self theory, and least so in anomie theory. It signifies the following:

(1) Human action does not typically happen all at once. It grows, it develops, it has a history. Although one stage may be a necessary antecedent to another, movement from one stage to another is not wholly determined by the antecedents. No one has put it better than Becker:

> . . . we need a model which takes into account the fact that patterns of behavior *develop* in orderly sequence. . . . We need, for example, one kind of explanation of how a person comes to be in a situation where marihuana is easily available to him, and another kind of explanation of why, given the fact of its availability, he is willing to experiment with it in the first place. And we need still another explanation of why, having experimented with it, he continues to use it. In a sense, each explanation constitutes a necessary cause of the behavior. That is, no one could become a confirmed marihuana user without going through each step. He must have the drug available, experiment with it, and continue to use it. The explanation of each step is thus part of the explanation of the resulting behavior.
>
> Yet the variables which account for each step may not, taken separately, distinguish between users and nonusers. The variable which disposes a person to take a particular step may not operate because he has not yet reached the stage in the process where it is possible to take that step.[15]

(2) The circumstances that determine movement along a particular path include both properties of the person and properties of the situation. There is probably no course of action that could not continue along more than one path, depending on the situation. On the other hand, there is probably no situation that could not elicit more than one response, depending on how the actor has been "prepared" by his experience in earlier stages of the developing course of action.

(3) Some of the circumstances that help to determine the development of the course of action are quite independent of events at earlier stages; some are outgrowths, often unanticipated, of events in earlier stages. For example, a person might set out to burglarize a house. Quite unexpectedly, the householder may come home and attack the burglar with a deadly weapon. The burglar, to save his own life, kills his attacker. What started out as a burglary might end up as a murder, due to a circumstance that was not necessarily implicit in the earlier stage of the act. However, although the arrival of the householder was a separately determined event, unforeseen and perhaps unforeseeable, the situation as a whole is partly a product of the actor's own doing. Householders do not typically assault invited guests with deadly weapons. This is why the law will not entertain in this instance the usual plea of justifiable homicide on grounds of self-defense.

Short and Strodtbeck, reporting on their research on delinquent gangs in Chicago, give similar examples and interpret them in similar terms. Delinquent cultures, they observe, frequently lead to delinquent actions not because they directly incite people to go out and do these things, malice well aforethought, but because they encourage them to put themselves into situations in which there is a heightened risk that *somebody else* might do something that will in turn precipitate a delinquent act. The participant in this culture might well be aware that the situation *could* develop in a certain way, and might earnestly wish that it would not. However, the attractions of the situation—*e.g.*, the status gains— might be so immediate and certain, and the risk of the undesired development

---

[15] Howard S. Becker, *Outsiders: Studies in the Sociology of Deviance* (New York: The Free Press of Glencoe, 1963), p. 23.

might seem (and from an actuarial standpoint might *be*) so small, that the risk is a small deterrent.[16]

(4) The situational component in the interaction process consists largely of feedback from other actors. How the action develops depends upon who witnesses and who is affected by the action, the perspectives through which they view it, and how they respond to it. Much of the literature that is concerned with the acquisition of and commitment to deviant roles is couched in essentially these terms: somebody, for any one of many reasons, does something that is in no sense "characteristic" or "distinctive" of him as contrasted to a multitude of other people. This behavior, however, lends itself to interpretation as a sign of a "deviant character." Whether it will be interpreted in this way, and the individual identified and labeled as that kind of a person, depends on who sees it and whether he is motivated to take action. Whether the label will stick, and the actor invested with the role, will depend partly on the reputation he has previously established and partly on the authority of those who apply the definition. To the extent that this definition becomes part of this public identity, the behavior of his publics might change in such a way that he no longer has the options available to him that he had before. He may be denied the opportunity to perform in ways that would effectively deny the role that has been imputed to him, or performance that would once have been above suspicion is now open to sinister interpretation. As options become more limited, or legitimate options more costly, the actor may drift [17] in the direction of behavior compatible with the stigmatized role. This behavior is likely to be interpreted as confirmation of the previous "diagnosis," and to result in a still sharper curtailment of options, which leads to still further commitment to the deviant role. During this process the actor may come to discover the satisfactions and profit that can be extracted from this role, or at least how to live comfortably with it, and may acquire new reference objects who will support him in his deviance. He may come, indeed, to accept the new role as part of his self—that is, to see himself, as others now do, as "somebody who acts in such and such a way," and possibly as somebody who "can't help" acting in this way.

This kind of analysis was applied to the interpretation of juvenile delinquency almost 30 years ago in a brilliant but greatly neglected classic of criminology of Frank Tannenbaum.[18] As we intimated in Chapter 3 (pp. 29-30), there has been a greatly increased research interest in recent years in the responses of the actor's milieu to his behavior, real or imaginary, and their consequences for the development of the actor's public identity and later career.

Just as deviance may be expressive or supportive of a role, so may responses to deviance. Action in *any* role, whether inside or outside the manifest structure of control, carries messages about the role incumbent and his adequacy to the role. Individuals may respond to deviance harshly, repressively, punitively, indignantly, tolerantly, understandingly, patiently, clinically, forgivingly, gently but firmly, and by turning the other cheek. We ordinarily chalk this up to individual differences, a product of their own past socialization, and let it go at that. But it may be more than that. It may derive much of its motivation from a need to communicate or to prove to others what kind of person one is.

I spent one summer as a member of the senior clinical staff of a treatment

---

[16] James F. Short, Jr., and Fred L. Strodtbeck, *Group Process and Gang Delinquency* (Chicago: The University of Chicago Press, 1965) Chaps. 2, 8, 11, and 12. Chapters 11 and 12 contain the clearest statement available of the points made in these two paragraphs.
[17] See the elaboration of the concept "drift" in David Matza, *Delinquency and Drift* (New York: Wiley, 1964).
[18] Frank Tannenbaum, *Crime and the Community* (Boston: Ginn, 1938).

culture, role, and interaction process

camp for emotionally disturbed children. The junior staff consisted of college students training for work with children as teachers, social workers, psychologists, and sociologists. For these students the situation was initially largely "unstructured"; they did not know how they were supposed to respond to the provocative behavior of the youngsters in their own roles as "clinicians." These expectations were defined for them by the senior staff. They included the ways in which a clinician is supposed to *define* the behavior of his charges, how he is supposed to *feel* about it, and what he is supposed to *do* about it. They were expected to see the children as victims of uncontrollable impulses somehow related to their harsh and depriving backgrounds, and in need of enormous doses of kindliness and indulgence in order to break down their images of the adult world as hateful and hostile. The clinician must never respond in anger or with intent to punish, although he might sometimes have to restrain or even isolate children in order to prevent them from hurting themselves or one another. Above all, the staff were expected to be warm and loving and always to be governed by a "clinical attitude"—that is, to respond in terms of what was therapeutically appropriate rather than in terms of their own notions of morality or emotional needs. This demanded of the junior staff what would ordinarily be regarded as superhuman patience in the face of intolerable provocation.

To an extraordinary degree, they fulfilled these expectations, including, I am convinced, the expectation that they *feel* sympathy and tenderness and love toward their charges, despite their animal-like behavior. The speed with which these college students learned to behave in this way cannot be easily explained in terms of gradual learning through a slow process of "internalization." They did, however, have a tremendous investment in their clinical roles. This investment was partly a product of their isolation, for a period of eight weeks, from the outside world, so that there were no seriously competing roles. Because of this isolation and the inexperience of the junior staff, the authority of the senior staff as reference group was unchallenged. These and other features of the social organization created a powerful need to demonstrate, to themselves and others, that they were authentic clinicians as defined by the senior staff. They had made certain claims about themselves, they had learned what constituted evidence of those claims, and they produced that evidence by behaving in a "clinical" manner.

In all probability, however, their conformity to the expectations of the clinical role was more than merely role-expressive behavior. Their assumption of the clinical role and their effort to live up to it were also instrumental to other roles. They were, after all, students, looking forward to graduation, to jobs, and to graduate school. They were being evaluated by the senior staff, and the impressions they made would become part of their "record," which could be used for or against them at later stages in their careers. Therefore, even though there might be no primary involvement or identification with the clinical role, "clinically appropriate" behavior was *supportive* of still other roles.

But we do not need to go so far afield, to seek such dramatic illustrations, or to limit ourselves to professional roles. We also have conceptions of how parents, Unitarians, liberals, patriotic Americans, intellectuals, God-fearing people, sophisticates, socially conscious people, and company commanders, among others, ought to feel and act about certain kinds of deviant behavior, or the deviant behavior of certain kinds of people (for example, children, underdogs, white-collar criminals, policemen, communists, drug addicts, basic trainees, and others). We also have our "personal roles": somebody who is "understanding," demands much of himself and demands the same of others," "never carries a grudge," "never flies off the handle," "knows a lot about psychology." How we will label others and respond to their deviant actions is partly determined by our investments in

105

these roles and the behavior that validates them. Probably we will also scrutinize and check our feelings to make sure that they are appropriate to the selves we claim or seek.

(5) This conception of interaction process applies to most social and cultural forms: the development and transformations of specific acts, whether they be individual or group enterprises; the ongoing, lifelong activity of building a self and acquiring a public identity; the establishment of networks of moral, emotional, and material interdependence and the creation of cooperative groups; and the emergence of cultural systems—*i.e.*, knowledge, beliefs, techniques, vocabularies, role classifications, and norms held in common and transmitted through communication. This statement is not meant to be a law of nature. There are no doubt events that build up swiftly and come rapidly to a head; that resemble an abrupt and discontinuous leap from one state or direction to another. But we are speaking of the way things usually happen: we muddle, we drift, we sniff the wind, we feel our way along, we hesitate, we forge ahead, we backtrack. Sometimes we plunge, because we must decide and the choices are few; but we arrive at such junctures, more often than not, by slow, small steps.

culture, role, and interaction process

converging trends
and
future prospects

ten

A study of my own, previously cited in connection with "mechanisms of defense," is a step toward the convergence of the diverse theoretical traditions we have considered.[1] I was struck by the failure of the cultural transmission theory to cope with the questions: "Why is there a delinquent culture to be transmitted?" "Why does it have the content that it does and why is it distributed as it is?" I set out the beginnings of a general theory of how subcultures come into existence, and applied it to the delinquent subculture. The structure of the larger system, its culture and social organization, create for people at each position in the system characteristic problems of adjustment and equip them, well or poorly, with the means for coping with them. Where the means for coping within the framework of the institutionalized norms are insufficient, or the occupants of these positions poorly equipped to take advantage of them, they will tend to reject those aspects of the culture that contribute to the creation of the problems or the barriers to their solution, and to substitute aspirations and norms they can live with more comfortably. When the problem is one (as it so often is) of achieving status and self-respect by the conventional criteria for measuring a person's worth, the response tends to take the form of substituting new criteria that they *can* meet. These criteria may permit or require behavior that violates the norms of conventional society; they may justify or demand deviant behavior.

To this point I had added little to what is explicit in Merton's paper, "Social Structure and Anomie." I went on, however, to stress that an acceptable solution must be one that commands the support of one's reference objects. To act on premises that nobody else shares is to isolate oneself, to invite punishment, and to consign oneself to doubt and uncertainty. Furthermore, to the degree that the

[1] Albert K. Cohen, *Delinquent Boys: The Culture of the Gang* (Glencoe, Ill.: The Free Press, 1955). See above, pp. 65–66.

problem is one of status, it is a problem of achieving recognition or acceptance by other people, and on their terms. A successful solution, therefore, requires a collective response. A number of people, each of whom functions as a reference object for the others, must jointly arrive at a new set of criteria and apply these criteria to one another. For this to happen, people with similar problems, people "in the same boat" because they occupy similar positions in the social structure, must be able to locate one another and communicate with one another. They can then sound one another out, make tentative and exploratory moves in new directions, experience the feedback, and—if the feedback is encouraging—go on to elaborate what becomes a new and in some respects deviant subculture. In persuading one another through this "conversation of gestures," one creates social support for his own inclinations, and thereby helps to persuade himself. Here we see the emphasis on the collective dimension of deviant behavior, characteristic of the cultural-transmission school, fused with the anomie tradition's emphasis on the distribution of socially structured strain, and the means for coping with it.

The delinquent subculture, I suggested, is a special case of a collective solution to a shared problem. In our discussion of psychodynamic mechanisms (see pp. 65-66) we reviewed my argument, which we will not repeat here, about the functions that delinquency performs for participants in this subculture. We omitted from this review, however, one of the central theses of my book: that it is precisely its subculture quality that makes it possible for delinquency to perform these functions. Were it not for the fact that its meaning is shared and ratified by a community of like-minded individuals, it would lack the stamp of legitimacy and it could not function as a criterion of status within the group, and as a basis for self-respect. We have already remarked that my interpretation of the meaning of delinquency has been severely criticized.[2] However, the critics have not taken similar exception to the more general theory of subcultures, of which the explanation of delinquency is a special application.

Illegitimate Opportunities:
Determinants of Response to Strain

Cloward and Ohlin

In a rather different way, the work of Cloward and Ohlin brings together the cultural transmission, role theory, and anomie traditions.[3] They note, as others have, that although Merton has a good deal to say on the sources of strain and on the variety of possible responses, he has relatively little to say about the determinants of this or that response. The concept of "illegitimate opportunity" is an attempt to remedy this deficiency. Not only are legitimate opportunities—i.e., access to normatively acceptable means—differentially distributed in the social structure; so are opportunities to achieve cultural goals by

[2] See especially John I. Kitsuse and David C. Dietrick, "Delinquent Boys: A Critique," *American Sociological Review* (April 1959), 24:208–215; Gresham Sykes and David Matza, "Techniques of Neutralization: A Theory of Delinquency," *American Sociological Review* (December 1957), 22:664–670; James F. Short, Jr. and Fred L. Strodtbeck, *Group Process and Gang Delinquency* (Chicago: The University of Chicago Press, 1965); and Walter Miller, "Lower Class Culture as a Generating Milieu of Gang Delinquency," *The Journal of Social Issues* (1958), 14:5–19.

[3] Richard A. Cloward, "Illegitimate Means, Anomie, and Deviant Behavior," *American Sociological Review* (April 1959), 24:164–176; and Richard A. Cloward, *et al.*, "Social Control in the Prison," *Theoretical Studies in Social Organization of the Prison* (New York: Social Science Research Council, March 1960); Richard A. Cloward and Lloyd B. Ohlin, *Delinquency and Opportunity: A Theory of Delinquent Gangs* (Glencoe, Ill.: The Free Press, 1960).

illegitimate means. Like myself, they assume that deviant responses typically take a subcultural form, but whether a deviant subculture will arise and what form it will take depends on the position of those who are subject to strain relative to the structure of illegitimate opportunities. This structure consists largely of the opportunity to learn, to practice, and to perform deviant roles. More specifically, it implies a milieu which contains models of successful deviance, opportunities to associate with and enjoy the tutelage of such models, and a setting which provides the agents and facilities necessary to make the deviance practicable and rewarding. The kinds of illegitimate opportunities and their distribution will determine the content of the deviant subculture. Here Merton's anomie theory is explicitly linked up to the traditional emphases of the Chicago school.

Delinquent subcultures, according to Cloward and Ohlin, typically take one of three forms: the criminal, the conflict, and the retreatist. The first emphasizes orderly, disciplined, rational activity oriented to economic gain; the second violence and gang fighting; the third drug use and other "kicks." The first tends to arise in areas where successful, big-time criminals reside, are accepted, and participate in conventional groups, and have reached a mutually acceptable and profitable accommodation with political machines and law-enforcement officials. Because they have a stake in an orderly and stable community—they raise their families there and may be pillars of the church!—they use their prestige and power to contain and discourage violence. Because they are leaders of successful criminal enterprises, they are on the alert for skillful, cool-headed reliable recruits. In such neighborhoods delinquency, responding to the illegitimate opportunity structure, takes on a flavor of apprenticeship for professional crime.

In neighborhoods where crime is small-time, petty, unsuccessful, and unglamorous, where there is no alliance between conventional and criminal elements, where the adult community in general is disunited and impotent, nobody is in a position to exercise effective control over the young people, and nobody can hold up to them promises of glittering rewards for either criminal or conventional careers. In such neighborhoods, young people tend to organize themselves in a community of gangs contending with one another for "rep" through the show of violence and toughness. In some communities, however, and among some of the young people in any community, neither of these delinquent opportunities is available. The barriers might be external, such as harshly repressive police measures that make street fighting too dangerous; or internal, such as moral or other inhibitions against the use of violence. Individuals denied access to criminal *and* conflict opportunities tend to withdraw into a world of their own that de-emphasizes both the serious concerns of the adult world (be they criminal or conventional) and the use of violence. This "world" emphasizes rather a "cool," "hip," cynical style of life and the cultivation of rare, intense, and immediate experiences, such as the "kicks" that narcotics provide. Although this theory of delinquent subcultures has thus far received only limited support from empirical research,[4] opportunity-structure theory, as the more general theory has come to be called, has revitalized and greatly enlarged the potentialities of anomie theory.

A Digression on the Concept
of Illegitimate Opportunity
The notion that there are two kinds of opportunity, legitimate and illegitimate, is not so simple as it seems. The distinction, although real, is "analytical" rather than "concrete." That is to say, there are not *some* things

---

[4] See Short and Strodtbeck, *op. cit.*, and Alfred R. Lindesmith and John H. Gagnon, "Anomie and Drug Addiction," in Marshall B. Clinard (ed.), *Anomie and Deviant Behavior* (New York: The Free Press of Glencoe, 1964), pp. 158–188.

109

that are legitimate opportunities and *other* things that are illegitimate opportunities, but the *same* things are typically, and perhaps always, both. A very simple example illustrates a point of very great generality. Identical firearms can be used to kill deer in season, or deer, policemen, and estranged spouses out of season. It is one of the most fundamental and pervasive dilemmas of social life that all legitimate power, whether over things or people, can be used to implement or to violate social norms.

One of the most familiar forms of the dilemma is that of organizational discretion. As we have remarked elsewhere, no set of rules can prescribe in exhaustive detail the duties of any office. There *must* be some range of legitimate discretion, some room for the exercise of judgment, if the obejctives of the rules are to be realized, for rarely are two situations in all relevant respects identical. The range of legitimate discretion that is necessary is highly variable; a doctor obviously requires more discretion than a postal clerk. But this is not important for our present purposes.

What does discretion mean? It means that within some limits a person is free to decide what he shall do, on the assumption that he will do the right thing. He will not be subject to minute surveillance or his motives scrutinized. This means also that every grant of discretion is a calculated or uncalculated risk. The discretion may always, again within some limits, be abused. Blau, in a study we have already referred to, notes that receptionists and interviewers in a state employment office were given a certain amount of discretion with respect to the re-appointment dates they set up with clients, in order that they might take into account such factors as "his occupation, his eagerness to work, his qualifications, present and prospective labor-market conditions, etc." [5] But this same discretion created the possibility of decisions based on criteria not authorized by the rules. For example, Blau also comments in a footnote:

> The applicant's chance of being interviewed, and thus of possibly getting a job, depended to some extent on the good will of the receptionist. Discretion opens the door to the possibility of discrimination. Indeed, as the discussion in ch. v will show, some ethnic discrimination occurred at the reception desk.[6]

The variety of illegitimate ends to which discretion can be turned is as diverse as the variety of human interests. It can be used to advance oneself in the organization or to secure one's position; as a weapon in interpersonal conflicts and rivalries; to do favors in exchange for favors, which is separated by a thin line from bribery; to promote the interests of other, perhaps rival organizations; to enforce illegitimate demands upon those affected by the exercise of discretion.

But the duties of *every* office, even where there is no explicit grant of discretion, confer opportunities for deviance. At the very least, they provide access, which others are denied, to restricted places, persons, objects, and information. The cookie jar may be taboo, but the keys to the pantry are the keys to the cookie jar. The prison guard must do business with the prisoner; the business transacted may not be contemplated by the rules. Mailmen must handle mail, and therefore other people's valuables. The delivery man or the meter reader, while going about their lawful appointed rounds, may collect the kinds of information that burglars value. The engineer in the research department of an industrial organization cannot help learning secrets of value to rival organizations, and therefore commodities that lend themselves to illicit exchange. The police power provides, in the interest of

---

[5] Blau, *The Dynamics of Bureaucracy* (Chicago: The University of Chicago Press, 1955), p. 28.

[6] *Ibid.*, p. 230, *f.n.* 11.

converging trends and future prospects

social control, access to all four restricted categories. So do agencies set up to exercise surveillance over the police power. In short, every structure of authority or responsibility is a structure of illegitimate opportunity.

Finally, all property, whether organizational or "private," is a socially recognized right, invariably hedged by socially recognized restrictions, to control over things; but with the right goes the power to exercise this control for unacceptable purposes. The dilemma is nicely illustrated by the effort of the socialist government of the Soviet Union to deal with a social problem by making a limited concession to the institution of private property:

> To try to ease the housing shortage, the Government decided to extend loans to private citizens who then could build their own homes. Soviet papers say that the result was that many people began to make a business out of it by renting rooms in their homes, or even renting the whole house while they stayed in the apartment that had been allocated to them by the state. Loans to private home builders have been stopped.[7]

The nature of the dilemma is further clarified by considering some of the structural devices to reduce the illegitimate exercise of discretion. Each of them works to a certain extent, but each of them has its price. (1) Discretion itself may be reduced, and replaced by detailed rules prescribing what shall be done in specific situations. (2) Supervision and surveillance may be increased. (3) Sanctions for the abuse of discretion may be made more severe. (4) Occupants of positions may be required to divest themselves of interests that may conflict with the interests that the discretion is designed to serve. For example, government officials may be required to sever their connections with their business firms or to dispose of their stock.

As we have already indicated, however, the reduction of discretion may entail a loss of organizational flexibility. To increase supervision and surveillance may be destructive of morale, especially where autonomy and trust are interpreted, as they usually are, as signs of status. To increase punishment can induce timorousness in the exercise of discretion, foster ritualism, and encourage the practice of "passing the buck." To require divestiture of potentially conflicting interests may discourage qualified persons from accepting positions.

Where reduction of discretion and coercive means of control (supervision, surveillance, and punishment) are ineffective or too costly, organizations tend to meet the problem by manning their positions with persons whose interests and values are compatible with the legitimate expectations of the organizational roles. The organizational devices for accomplishing this are rigorous selection according to this criterion during the recruitment process, and intensive socialization after recruitment.[8] There are more and less effective ways of dealing with the dilemma, according to the circumstances, but it is never wholly resolved. Deviance can usually be reduced at a cost that is not intolerable, but any means that would expunge it completely would probably be destructive of any organization.

Interaction Process
and Anomie Theory
Interaction process implies that an actor's initial move alters his environment and thereby the conditions that affect his next move. However, such a general statement does not tell us much about the actual unfolding

---

[7] *U.S. News and World Report*, June 12, 1961, p. 49.

[8] For a more extended discussion of this point, see another volume in this series, Amitai Etzioni, *Modern Organizations* (Englewood Cliffs, New Jersey: Prentice-Hall, 1964), pp. 68–74.

111

of the interaction process. It is necessary to translate this process into the language of some conceptual scheme that will enable us to grasp more precisely the relationship between the various stages in this process. In this section we will suggest some directions for further exploration, taking the language of anomie theory as our starting point.[9]

In anomie theory the situation is conceptualized in terms of a structure of opportunity, and the actor's response in terms of acceptance and rejection of goals and means. What the actor does, however, is an aspect of the situation of action for other actors. It may be fruitful to ask, "How does his act affect *their* opportunity structures?" This depends, of course, on their roles and the activities in which they are engaged; it will therefore have different consequences for different people. For example, an illegal conspiracy in restraint of trade will affect in quite different ways the opportunity structures of competitors who are not part of the conspiracy, of those of the consuming public, and of those of agencies charged with enforcement of fair competition. Furthermore, bearing in mind our observations in the last section, the same event may affect both the legitimate and illegitimate opportunities of the same people. For example, officials of regulatory agencies may find their enforcement assignments more difficult, but they may also see in this conspiracy an opportunity to exploit the conspirators in exchange for nonenforcement. In like manner, the cheater where the instructor grades on a curve poses one problem for the instructor and another for the students who are too honest or too fearful to cheat. A special case of great interest, suggested by role theory, is that in which the deviant provides others with opportunities to present themselves in roles with which they would like to be identified, such as martyrs, clinicians, crusaders, or even professional students of deviance.

What other people will then do can also be formulated in anomie terms. On the one hand, the culture structure specifies for each role *what* the incumbent is supposed to do about deviance and *how* he is supposed to go about it—his goals and the institutionalized means. If somebody is attacked in a public place, the cultural prescriptions are different for the policeman, a kinsman of the victim, and unrelated bystanders. If someone observes a student cheating, the prescriptions are different if the observer is the instructor and if he is a fellow student, although in both cases the prescriptions may be ambiguous and uncertain. Assuming that they are reasonably clear, the *responses* to deviance can then be formulated in terms of Merton's typology. One may see one's duty and do it (Conformity). If the institutionalized means seem insufficient or unduly troublesome, as is so often the case in law enforcement, he may resort to illegitimate means, if these are available (Innovation). He may "go by the book," without regard to the end in view (Ritualism), and so on. The legitimacy of his response may in turn affect the responses of third parties or the subsequent actions of the deviant. Where, for example, a policeman or a parent employs, or is believed to employ, unnecessary brutality, third parties may side with the offender, and the offender, rather than "take his medicine," may resist.

The response to deviance may be conceptualized not only in such normative terms but also in terms of what it, in turn, does to the opportunity structure of the offender. It may open up new legitimate opportunities or it may close them off. (We considered the latter possibility in our analysis, in Chapter 3, of the transformation of the offender into a deviant character.) It may also open up or close off illegitimate opportunities. In brief, looking at the interaction from the point of view of either party to the process, the implications for him of what the

---

[9] This section is largely adapted from somewhat more extended remarks in Albert K. Cohen, "The Sociology of the Deviant Act: Anomie Theory and Beyond," *American Sociological Review* (February 1965), 30:9–14.

112

other party does can be represented by means of a fourfold table. (For example, a parent might buy his teen-age son a jalopy of his own in order to discourage "borrowing" of the family car. This would be an example of "Opens up legitimate opportunities," represented by the box in the upper left-hand corner.) This change in the opportunity structure helps to determine his next move.

	Legitimate Opportunities	Illegitimate Opportunities
Opens up		
Closes off		

Consider, for example, the following excerpt from Sutherland and Cressey's treatment of the development of techniques of crime and of protection against crime:

> When the police develop an invention for the detection or identification of criminals, the criminals utilize a device to protect themselves. When the police began to use the fingerprint technique, criminals began to wear gloves and to wipe surfaces that had been touched by them. The police utilize the radio to notify squad cars of the location of a crime that is being committed and to direct those cars in the pursuit of criminals. The well-equipped burglars carry their own short-wave radio sets with them, tune them in while they are at work, and are informed of an alarm as quickly as are the police. The police are trying to perfect selective devices for radio calls which will restrict the calls to police cars, but it may be expected that if this difficulty develops the criminals will devise methods of overcoming it.[10]

This passage, and the longer treatment from which it is taken, was arrived at without benefit of anomie theory, but it can readily be translated into terms of an interaction process between two opportunity structures. The advantage of approaching data with such a conceptual scheme explicitly in mind is that it forcibly directs attention to certain kinds of interconnections and developmental processes. It thereby increases the likelihood of their discovery and reduces dependence upon accidental insight and informed but unsystematic intuition.

Deviance Theories and Social Control

In the section immediately preceding, we started from a theory of deviance, applied its terms to both sides of the interaction process, and tried to characterize, within the terms of that theory, both the processes engendering deviance and those tending to reduce it. In other words, we have extended its scope so that we now have the beginnings of a unified theory of deviance and the social control of deviance. Formulated in this way, the theory suggests possible ways of deliberately and self-consciously intervening for purposes of social control, and of analyzing and appraising existing or proposed programs of social control. The same approach can be readily extended to other theories of deviance. In Chapter 9, for example, we have already suggested that *both* parties to the interaction process can be characterized in terms of the kinds of selves they are seeking to establish, and in terms of the role-expressive and role-supportive nature

[10] Edwin H. Sutherland and Donald R. Cressey, *Principles of Criminology*, 6th ed. (Chicago: Lippincott, 1960), p. 225.

of their responses to the acts of the other party. Were we to start from differential association theory as a special case of cultural transmission theory, we would attempt to formulate the responses of the milieu in terms of (a) transformations in the cultural content of the milieu itself, including the impact upon the milieu of *its* associations with the actor, and (b) changes in those properties of the relationship between the actor and his milieu affecting the frequency, priority, duration, and intensity of association with pro-deviant and anti-deviant associations. In terms of deliberately contrived efforts at control, programs emphasizing the first would be illustrated by attempts to transform, through "guided group interaction," [11] a delinquent into an anti-delinquent subculture. The latter would be illustrated by efforts of probation officers, directly through the exercise of their authority over the child, or indirectly through counseling parents concerning the exercise of their influence and authority, to supervise and redirect the associations of the child.

It is beyond the scope of a book no larger than this to examine in detail, from this point of view, concrete programs for the social control of deviance. We have concentrated, rather, on setting forth the general theories that would provide the basis for such an examination. However, a couple of general comments are in order. First, it does not necessarily follow directly, from a unified theory of deviance and control, how one goes about deliberately structuring the interaction process so as to manipulate, in the desired way, the variables affecting the production and reduction of deviance. So, for example, it is not obvious how one goes about transforming a subculture, or opening up legitimate opportunities, or creating a milieu that will respond to the deviant in such a way that the deviant's response, in turn, will be an "increase in ego strength," if these are the changes that the theories seem to call for. Second, if we can assume that a certain program is demonstrably effective in reducing deviance, the results can often be interpreted in terms of more than one theory. For example, if detached work with boys' gangs clearly reduces delinquency, the results can be—and have been—attributed to the success of the leader (1) in opening up new opportunities for gratifying nondelinquent activities; (2) in transmitting his own values to the boys through differential association; (3) as a therapist, in helping the boys to work through their respective problems of adjustment and rendering delinquency, as a mechanism of defense, unnecessary; and (4), as a cultural engineer, so to speak, in manipulating the interaction process within the group so as to effect a change in the group culture. Our point is not that it is impossible to determine which process or processes are at work; it is to re-emphasize that, although general theories of deviance and control have important implications for the design and evaluation of control programs, they do not of themselves (see pp. 37-38) provide final and detailed solutions.

[11] LaMar T. Empey and Jerome Rabow, "The Provo Experiment in Delinquency Rehabilitation," *American Sociological Review* (October 1961), 26:679–695. See also Donald R. Cressey, *Delinquency, Crime and Differential Association* (The Hague: Martinus Nijhoff, 1964), Chaps. 8 and 9.

selected references

The following three textbooks are general introductions to the field of "social problems" or "social disorganization," which is broader than deviant behavior as we understand it here. However, each contains useful general observations on the sociology of deviant behavior as well as excellent chapters on particular kinds of deviance: Edwin M. Lemert, *Social Pathology* (New York: McGraw-Hill, 1951); Marshall B. Clinard, *Sociology of Deviant Behavior*, rev. ed. (New York: Holt, Rinehart and Winston, 1963); and Robert K. Merton and Robert A. Nisbet (eds.), *Contemporary Social Problems*, rev. ed. (New York: Harcourt, Brace and World, 1966).

Crime and juvenile delinquency, on the other hand, are not so broad as deviant behavior; however, a large part of deviance theory has its origins in criminology. Two good criminology textbooks are Edwin H. Sutherland and Donald R. Cressey, *Principles of Criminology*, 6th ed. (Philadelphia: Lippincott, 1960); and Richard R. Korn and Lloyd W. McCorkle, *Criminology and Penology* (New York: Holt, 1959). Useful readers in this area are Norman Johnston, Leonard Savitz, and Marvin E. Wolfgang (eds.), *The Sociology of Punishment and Correction* (New York: Wiley, 1962); Marvin E. Wolfgang, Leonard Savitz, and Norman Johnston (eds.), *The Sociology of Crime and Delinquency* (New York: Wiley, 1962); Gus Tyler (ed), *Organized Crime in America* (Ann Arbor: University of Michigan Press, 1962); and Sheldon Glueck (ed.), *The Problem of Delinquency* (Boston: Houghton Mifflin, 1959).

The following present or appraise theories and concepts applicable to a wide spectrum of deviant behavior: Talcott Parsons, "Deviant Behavior and the Mechanisms of Social Control," in *The Social System* (Glencoe, Ill.: The Free Press, 1951), Chap. 7; Albert K. Cohen, "The Study of Social Disorganization and Deviant Behavior," in Robert K. Merton, Leonard Broom, and Leonard S. Cottrell (eds.), *Sociology Today: Problems and Prospects* (New York: Basic Books, 1959), Chap. 21; Harry M. Johnson, "Social Conformity, Social Deviation, and its Control," in *Sociology: A Systematic Introduction* (New York: Harcourt, Brace and World, 1960), Chap. 20; Judith Blake and Kingsley Davis, "Norms, Values, and Sanctions," in Robert E. L. Faris (ed.), *Handbook of Modern Sociology* (Chicago: Rand, McNally, 1964), Chap. 13; and Edwin M. Schur, *Crimes Without Victims: Deviant Behavior and Public Policy* (Englewood Cliffs, N.J.: Prentice-Hall, 1965).

The major works of the anomie tradition are Emile Durkheim, *Suicide*, trans. by John A. Spaulding and George Simpson (Glencoe, Ill.: The Free Press, 1951); Robert K. Merton, *Social Theory and Social Structure*, rev. ed. (Glencoe, Ill.: The Free Press, 1957), Chaps. 4 and 5; Richard A. Cloward and Lloyd E. Ohlin, *Delinquency and Opportunity* (Glencoe, Ill.: The Free Press, 1960); and Marshall B. Clinard (ed.), *Anomie and Deviant Behavior: A Discussion and Critique* (New York: The Free Press of Glencoe, 1964).

The classics of the Chicago tradition are William I. Thomas and Florian Znaniecki, *The Polish Peasant in Europe and America* (New York: Dover Publications, 1958), especially Vol. 2, Part 2; and George Herbert Mead, *Mind, Self, and Society* (Chicago: University of Chicago Press, 1934). The latter does not deal specifically with deviance, but it is the leading source of modern ideas on role theory and the self. Important contemporary works are Erving Goffman, *Stigma: Notes on the Management of Spoiled Identity* (Englewood Cliffs, N.J.: Prentice-Hall, 1963); and Howard S. Becker, *Outsiders: Studies in the Sociology of Deviance* (New York: The Free Press of Glencoe, 1963). See also Frank Tannenbaum, *Crime and the Community* (Boston: Ginn, 1938); and Alfred R. Lindesmith, *Opiate Addiction* (Bloomington: Principia Press, 1947). For leading works in the cultural-transmission stream of the Chicago tradition, see references to Shaw and McKay, Sutherland, and Cressey on pp. 94-97 of this volume. Theories emphasizing internal controls, mechanisms of defense, personal pathology, and internal conflicts are illustrated by Franz Alexander and Hugo L. Staub, *The Criminal, The Judge, and the Public* (Glencoe, Ill.: The Free Press, 1956); William Healy and Augusta F. Bronner, *New Light on Delinquency and its Treatment* (New Haven: Yale University Press, 1938); Albert Bandura and Richard H. Walters, *Adolescent Aggression* (New York: Ronald, 1959); and Fritz Redl and David Wineman, *The Aggressive Child* (Glencoe, Ill.: The Free Press, 1957).

Studies on juvenile delinquency that have general import for deviance theory are Albert K. Cohen, *Delinquent Boys: The Culture of the Gang* (Glencoe, Ill.: The Free Press, 1955); Walter B. Miller, "Lower Class Culture as a Generating Milieu of Gang Delinquency," *Journal of Social Issues* (1958), 14:5-19; Cloward and Ohlin, cited above in connection with anomie theory; James F. Short, Jr.

and Fred L. Strodtbeck, *Group Process and Gang Delinquency* (Chicago: University of Chicago Press, 1965); and David Matza, *Delinquency and Drift* (New York: Wiley, 1964).

Most of the works cited on these pages deal at length with aspects of social control of deviant behavior. In addition, see Donald R. Cressey, *Delinquency, Crime and Differential Association* (The Hague: Martinus Nijhoff, 1964), Chaps. 8 and 9; Donald R. Cressey (ed.), *The Prison: Studies in Institutional Organization and Change* (New York: Holt, Rinehart and Winston, 1961); Jerome Hall, *Theft, Law and Society* (Boston: Little, Brown, 1935); George C. Homans, "Social Control," in *The Human Group* (New York: Harcourt, Brace, 1950), Chap. 11; Richard C. Donnelly, Joseph Goldstein, and Richard D. Schwartz (eds.), *Criminal Law* (New York: The Free Press of Glencoe, 1962); and Leslie T. Wilkins, *Social Deviance: Social Policy, Action, and Research* (Englewood Cliffs, N.J.: Prentice-Hall, 1965).

selected references

index

117

disorganization caused by, 4-6
functions for organization, 6-11
Merton's typology, 77
of collectivities, 21-23
reactions to, and group solidarity, 8-9
relativity to roles, 11-15
visibility of, 27-28
Deviant behavior, theories of:
anomie, 75-83, 102, 107-109, 111-113
bio-anthropological, 49-53
conjunctive, 44
control, 49 ff.
cultural transmission, 93-97
differential association, 95-97, 101
frustration-aggression, 57-58, 61
interaction process, 43-44, 101-106, 111-113
"kinds-of-people," 42, 70
levels and types of, 41-47
psychoanalytical instinct, 54-56
psychodynamic control, 54-55
psychological, 41
research strategies for, table, 42
role-self, 97-101
sociological, 45-46
Deviant character, 24, 29-30
Deviant roles, 32
Dietrick, David, 108n
Differential association, 95-97, 101
Discretion, illegitimate exercise of, 80, 110-111
Displacement, 63
Dollard, John, 57
Donnelly, Richard C., 22n
Doob, Leonard W., 57n
Drug addiction, 34-36, 66-67, 86-88
Dubin, Robert, 77n
Durkheim, Emile, 59, 101
anomie theory, 74-75
morality, 3
suicide, 46-47, 75

Ectomorphy, 51
Ego, 2, 57
Eissler, Kurt R., 57n
Embezzlement, 100
Empey, LaMar T., 25n, 114n
Endomorphy, 51
Enforcement agents, 28
Erickson, Maynard L., 25n
Erikson, Kai, 8, 10
Ethnic groups, delinquency and, 94-95
Eugenics, crime control and, 51

Federal Bureau of Narcotics, marihuana legislation, 35
Ferri, Enrico, 49
Finestone, Harold, 66
Freeman, Howard E., 14n
Freud, Sigmund, 57, 67
Frustration-aggression theory, 57-58, 61

Gagnon, John H., 109n
Gambling, 5
Gebhard, Paul H., 27n
Geiger, Kent, 82n
Gibbs, Jack, 58
Glueck, Sheldon and Eleanor, 52-53
Goffman, Erving, 36, 98, 99
Goldstein, Joseph, 22n
Goring, Charles, 50
Granick, David, 82n
Grosser, George, 99, 102

Hartl, Emil M., 51n
Hartmann, Heinz, 51n
Henry, Andrew F., 58
Heretics, 32
Hewitt, Lester E., 26, 55
Hobbes, Thomas, 2
Homans, George C. 89,
Homicide, suicide and, 58
Homosexuality (see Sexual deviance)
Hooton, Ernest A., 50-51
Hurwitz, Stephan, 53n

Id, 2, 55
Illegitimate opportunity, 108-111
Imputation, problems of, 60, 71
Individual adaptation, modes of, table, 77
Inkeles, Alex, 19n, 82n
Innovation, 77
Institutionalization, 19-21
Interaction process, 43-44, 101-106, 111-113

Jaspan, Norman, 6n
Jenkins, Richard L., 26n, 55
Johnson, Adelaide M., 56n
Johnson, Harry M., 15n, 19n
Juvenile delinquency:
as legal category, 32
Cohen theory, 65-66, 107-108
Cloward-Ohlin theory, 108-109
distribution, 94
Grosser role theory, 99
reaction-formation and, 65-66
relational dependence and, 85-86
somatypes and, 52
Juveniles, diminishing responsibility, 32

"Kinds-of-people" theories, 42, 70
bio-anthropological, 49
biological, 43
cultural-transmission, 93
Kitsuse, John I., 108n
Korn, Richard, 53n, 101
"Krugovaya poruka," 88-90

119